DANIEL
with an
INTRODUCTION TO APOCALYPTIC LITERATURE

JOHN J. COLLINS

The Forms of the Old Testament Literature
VOLUME XX
Rolf Knierim and Gene M. Tucker, editors

WILLIAM B. EERDMANS PUBLISHING COMPANY
GRAND RAPIDS, MICHIGAN

Copyright © 1984 by William B. Eerdmans Publishing Company
255 Jefferson Ave. S.E., Grand Rapids, MI 49503

Library of Congress Cataloging in Publication Data

Collins, John Joseph, 1946-
Daniel: with an introduction to apocalyptic literature.

(The Forms of the Old Testament literature; v. 20)
Includes bibliographical references.
1. Bible. O.T. Daniel—Commentaries. 2. Apocalyptic
literature—History and criticism. I. Title. II. Series.
BS1555.3.C64 1984   224'.507   84-13783

ISBN 0-8028-0020-3 (pbk.)

Reprinted, January 1989

CONTENTS

Abbreviations and Symbols

I. Miscellaneous abbreviations and symbols

Akk.	Akkadian
ca.	*circa* (about)
cf.	compare
ch(s).	chapter(s)
ed.	editor(s), edition
e.g.	for example
esp.	especially
et al.	*et alii* (and others)
Fest.	*Festschrift*
i.e.	*id est* (that is)
LXX	Septuagint
MS(S)	manuscript(s)
OT	Old Testament
p(p).	page(s)
repr.	reprint
tr.	translated by
v(v).	verse(s)
vol(s).	volume(s)
→	The arrow indicates a cross reference to another section of the commentary
§(§)	section(s)

II. Publications

AB	Anchor Bible
AnBib	Analecta biblica
ANET	J. B. Pritchard, ed., *Ancient Near Eastern Texts Relating to the Old Testament* (3rd ed.; Princeton: Princeton University Press, 1969)
ANRW	*Aufstieg und Niedergang der römischen Welt*

AnSt	Anatolian Studies
ArOr	*Archiv orientální*
ARW	*Archiv für Religionswissenschaft*
AUSS	*Andrews University Seminary Studies*
BASOR	*Bulletin of the American Schools of Oriental Research*
Bib	*Biblica*
BibS(N)	Biblische Studien (Neukirchen, 1951-)
BZ	*Biblische Zeitschrift*
BZAW	Beihefte zur Zeitschrift für die Alttestamentliche Wissenschaft
CBQ	*Catholic Biblical Quarterly*
CBQMS	Catholic Biblical Quarterly—Monograph Series
ConB	Coniectanea biblica
ETL	*Ephemerides theologicae lovanienses*
FOTL	The Forms of the Old Testament Literature
FRLANT	Forschungen zur Religion und Literatur des Alten und Neuen Testaments
HAT	Handbuch zum Alten Testament
HKAT	Handkommentar zum Alten Testament
HSM	Harvard Semitic Monographs
HTS	Harvard Theological Studies
HUCA	*Hebrew Union College Annual*
ICC	International Critical Commentary
IDBSup	*Interpreter's Dictionary of the Bible*, Supplementary volume
JAOS	*Journal of the American Oriental Society*
JBL	*Journal of Biblical Literature*
JQR	*Jewish Quarterly Review*
JSJ	*Journal for the Study of Judaism in the Persian, Hellenistic, and Roman Period*
JSOT	*Journal for the Study of the Old Testament*
JSOTSup	Journal for the Study of the Old Testament, Supplement Series
JTS	*Journal of Theological Studies*
KAT	Kommentar zum Alten Testament
LD	Lectio divina
NTAbh	Neutestamentliche Abhandlungen
NTS	*New Testament Studies*
OTL	Old Testament Library
OTS	*Oudtestamentische Studiën*
RB	*Revue biblique*

RevQ	*Revue de Qumran*
RSV	*Revised Standard Version*
RTL	*Revue théologique de Louvain*
SB	Sources bibliques
SBLASP	Society of Biblical Literature Abstracts and Seminar Papers
SBLDS	Society of Biblical Literature Dissertation Series
SBLMS	Society of Biblical Literature Monograph Series
SBT	Studies in Biblical Theology
Sem	*Semitica*
ST	*Studia theologica*
TDNT	G. Kittel and G. Friedrich, eds., *Theological Dictionary of the New Testament* (tr. and ed. G. Bromiley; 10 vols.; Grand Rapids: Eerdmans, 1964-1976)
ThStKr	*Theologische Studien und Kritiken*
TRu	*Theologische Rundschau*
TUMSR	Trinity University Monograph Series in Religion
USQR	*Union Seminary Quarterly Review*
VT	*Vetus Testamentum*
VTSup	Vetus Testamentum, Supplements
WMANT	Wissenschaftliche Monographien zum Alten und Neuen Testament
WUNT	Wissenschaftliche Untersuchungen zum Neuen Testament
ZA	*Zeitschrift für Assyriologie*
ZAW	*Zeitschrift für die alttestamentliche Wissenschaft*

EDITORS' FOREWORD

THIS BOOK is the fourth in a series of twenty-four volumes planned for publication throughout the nineteen-eighties. The series eventually will present a form-critical analysis of every book and each unit of the Old Testament (Hebrew Bible) according to a standard outline and methodology. The aims of the work are fundamentally exegetical, attempting to understand the biblical literature from the viewpoint of a particular set of questions. Each volume in the series will also give an account of the history of the form-critical discussion of the material in question, attempt to bring consistency to the terminology for the genres and formulas of the biblical literature, and expose the exegetical procedure in such a way as to enable students and pastors to engage in their own analysis and interpretation. It is hoped, therefore, that the audience will be a broad one, including not only biblical scholars but also students, pastors, priests, and rabbis who are engaged in biblical interpretation.

There is a difference between the planned order of appearance of the individual volumes and their position in the series. While the series follows basically the sequence of the books of the Hebrew Bible, the individual volumes will appear in accordance with the projected working schedules of the individual contributors. The number of twenty-four volumes has been chosen for merely practical reasons which make it necessary to combine several biblical books in one volume at times, and at times to have two authors contribute to the same volume. Volume XIII is an exception to the arrangement according to the sequence of the Hebrew canon in that it omits Lamentations. The commentary on Lamentations will be published with that on the book of Psalms.

The initiation of this series is the result of deliberations and plans which began some fifteen years ago. At that time the current editors perceived the need for a comprehensive reference work which would enable scholars and students of the Hebrew scriptures to gain from the insights that form-critical work had accumulated throughout seven decades, and at the same time to participate more effectively in such work themselves. An international and interconfessional team of scholars was assembled, and has been expanded in recent years.

Several possible approaches and formats for publication presented themselves. The work could not be a handbook of the form-critical method with some examples of its application. Nor would it be satisfactory to present an encyclopedia of the genres identified in the Old Testament literature. The reference work would have to demonstrate the method on all of the texts, and identify genres only through the actual interpretation of the texts themselves. Hence, the work had to be a commentary following the sequence of the books in the Hebrew Bible (the

Kittel edition of the *Biblia Hebraica* then and the *Biblia Hebraica Stuttgartensia* now).

The main purpose of this project is to lead the student to the Old Testament texts themselves, and not just to form-critical studies of the texts. It should be stressed that the commentary is confined to the form-critical interpretation of the texts. Consequently, the reader should not expect here a full-fledged exegetical commentary which deals with the broad range of issues concerning the meaning of the text. In order to keep the focus as clearly as possible on a particular set of questions, matters of text, translation, philology, verse-by-verse explanation, etc. are raised only when they appear directly relevant to the form-critical analysis and interpretation.

The adoption of a commentary format and specific methodological deliberations imply a conclusion which has become crucial for all the work of form criticism. If the results of form criticism are to be verifiable and generally intelligible, then the determination of typical forms and genres, their settings and functions, has to take place through the analysis of the forms in and of the texts themselves. This leads to two consequences for the volumes in this series. First, each interpretation of a text begins with the presentation of the *structure* of that text in outline form. The ensuing discussion of this structure attempts to distinguish the typical from the individual or unique elements, and to proceed on this basis to the determination of the *genre,* its *setting,* and its *intention.* Traditio-historical factors are discussed throughout this process where relevant; e.g., is there evidence of a written or oral stage of the material earlier than the actual text before the reader?

Second, the interpretation of the texts accepts the fundamental premise that we possess all texts basically at their latest written stages, technically speaking, at the levels of the final redactions. Any access to the texts, therefore, must confront and analyze that latest edition first, i.e., a specific version of that edition as represented in a particular text tradition. Consequently, the commentary proceeds from the analysis of the larger literary corpora created by the redactions back to any prior discernible stages in their literary history. Larger units are examined first, and then their subsections. Therefore, in most instances the first unit examined in terms of structure, genre, setting, and intention is the entire biblical book in question; next the commentary treats the individual larger and then smaller units.

The original plan of the project was to record critically all the relevant results of previous form-critical studies concerning the texts in question. While this remains one of the goals of the series, it had to be expanded to allow for more of the research of the individual contributors. This approach has proved to be important not only with regard to the ongoing insights of the contributors, but also in view of the significant developments which have taken place in the field in recent years. The team of scholars responsible for the series is committed to following a basic design throughout the commentary, but differences of emphasis and even to some extent of approach will be recognized as more volumes appear. Each author will ultimately be responsible for his own contribution.

The use of the commentary is by and large self-explanatory, but a few comments may prove helpful to the reader. This work is designed to be used alongside a Hebrew text or a translation of the Bible. The format of the interpretation of the texts, large or small, is the same throughout, except in cases where the biblical material itself suggests a different form of presentation. Individual books and major literary corpora are introduced by a general bibliography referring to wider information on the subjects discussed, and to works relevant for the subunits of that literary body. Whenever available, a special form-critical bibliography for a specific unit under discussion will conclude the discussion of that unit. In the outline of the structure of units, the system of sigla attempts to indicate the relationship and interdependence of the parts within that structure. The traditional chapter and verse divisions of the Hebrew text are supplied in the right-hand margin of the outlines. Where there is a difference between the Hebrew and English versification the latter is also supplied in parentheses according to the *Revised Standard Version*.

In addition to the commentary on the biblical book, this volume includes an introduction to the major genres found in the apocalyptic literature and a glossary of the genres discussed in the commentary. Most of the definitions in the glossary were prepared by Professor Collins, but some have arisen from the work of other members of the project on other parts of the Old Testament. Each subsequent volume will include such a glossary. Eventually, upon the completion of the commentary series, all of the glossaries will be revised in the light of the analysis of each book of the Old Testament and published as Volume XXIV of the series. The individual volumes will not contain special indices but the indices for the entire series will be published as Volume XXIII.

The editors wish to acknowledge with appreciation the contribution of numerous persons and institutions to the work of the project. All of the contributors have received significant financial, secretarial, and student assistance from their respective institutions. In particular, the editors have received extensive support from their Universities. Without such concrete expressions of encouragement the work scarcely could have gone on. At Claremont, the Institute for Antiquity and Christianity has from its own inception provided office facilities, a supportive staff, and the atmosphere which stimulates not only individual but also team research. Emory University and the Candler School of Theology have likewise provided tangible support and encouragement. The editors are particularly indebted to Elaine C. Hoffman-Fowler, student at Candler School of Theology, for her assistance in the editorial process.

ROLF KNIERIM
GENE M. TUCKER

PREFACE

I SHOULD like to acknowledge my indebtedness in the production of this book to my collaborators in the SBL Genres Project, Task Force on Apocalypses, 1975-79: Harry Attridge, Frank Fallon, Tony Saldarini, and Adela Yarbro Collins; to Gene Tucker for his stimulating editorial guidance; to Kent Richards for initially introducing me to the work of the FOTL project; and to the College of Liberal Arts and Sciences of DePaul University for a generous summer grant which facilitated the completion of the manuscript.

JOHN J. COLLINS
DePaul University

Introduction to
Apocalyptic
Literature

BIBLIOGRAPHY

D. E. Aune, *Prophecy in Early Christianity and the Ancient Mediterranean World* (Grand Rapids: Eerdmans, 1983) 107-21; J. Carmignac, "Qu'est-ce que l'Apocalyptique? Son emploi à Qumrân," *RevQ* 10 (1979) 3-33; J. J. Collins, ed., *Semeia 14: Apocalypse: The Morphology of a Genre* (Missoula: Scholars Press, 1979); idem, *The Apocalyptic Imagination in Ancient Judaism* (New York: Crossroad, 1984); J. G. Gammie, "The Classification, Stages of Growth, and Changing Intentions in the Book of Daniel," *JBL* 95 (1976) 191-204; P. D. Hanson, "Apocalypse, Genre," *IDBSup*; L. Hartman, "Survey of the Problem of Apocalyptic Genre," in *Apocalypticism in the Mediterranean World and the Near East* (ed. D. Hellholm; Tübingen: Mohr, 1983) 329-43; D. Hellholm, ed., *Apocalypticism in the Mediterranean World and the Near East* (Tübingen: Mohr, 1983); idem, *Das Visionenbuch des Hermas als Apokalypse: Formgeschichtliche und texttheoretische Studien zu einer literarischen Gattung* I (ConB 13/1; Lund: Gleerup, 1980); idem, "The Problem of Apocalyptic Genre and the Apocalypse of John," SBLASP 21 (1982) 157-98; K. Koch, *The Rediscovery of Apocalyptic* (tr. M. Kohl; SBT 2/22; Naperville: Allenson, 1972); K. Koch and J. M. Schmidt, eds., *Apokalyptik* (Darmstadt: Wissenschaftliche Buchgesellschaft, 1982); F. Lücke, *Versuch einer vollständigen Einleitung in die Offenbarung Johannis und in die gesamte apokalyptische Literatur* (Bonn: Weber, 1832); G. von Rad, *Theologie des Alten Testaments,* II (4th ed.; Munich: Chr. Kaiser, 1965); C. Rowland, *The Open Heaven: A Study of Apocalyptic in Judaism and Christianity* (New York: Crossroad, 1982); E. Sanders, "The Genre of Palestinian Jewish Apocalypses," in *Apocalypticism in the Mediterranean World and the Near East* (ed. D. Hellholm; Tübingen: Mohr, 1983) 447-59; J. M. Schmidt, *Die jüdische Apokalyptik* (Neukirchen-Vluyn: Neukirchener, 1969); H. Stegemann, "Die Bedeutung der Qumranfunde für die Erforschung der Apokalyptik," in *Apocalypticism in the Mediterranean World and the Near East* (ed. D. Hellholm; Tübingen: Mohr, 1983) 495-530; M. E. Stone, "Lists of Revealed Things in the Apocalyptic Literature," in *Magnalia Dei: The Mighty Acts of God (Fest.* G. E. Wright; ed. F. M. Cross, W. E. Lemke, and P. D. Miller, Jr.; Garden City: Doubleday, 1976) 439-43; P. Vielhauer, "Apocalypses and Related Subjects," in *New Testament Apocrypha* (ed. E. Hennecke and W. Schneemelcher; Philadelphia: Westminster, 1965) 2.581-607.

THE APOCALYPTIC literature has been recognized as a distinct class of writings since the work of Friedrich Lücke in the early nineteenth century. Yet there has been surprisingly little form-critical analysis of these documents. Apart from the general lack of detailed studies of the Pseudepigrapha, three factors have impeded progress in this area:

(1) The use of "apocalyptic" as a noun in English to refer to an amalgam

of literary, social, and phenomenological elements has engendered confusion. Since the work of Koch, Stone, and Hanson there has been widespread agreement that the genre apocalypse should be distinguished from "apocalypticism" and "apocalyptic eschatology."

(2) The genre apocalypse was not clearly recognized and labeled in antiquity. The use of "apocalypse" as a genre label appears to be derived from the book of Revelation in the NT. In the light of the Mani Codex, which speaks of "apocalypses" of Adam, Sethel, Enosh, Shem, Enoch, and Paul, it would seem that eventually the term was widely used to designate a class of writings. Among the Jewish apocalypses of the period 250 B.C. to A.D. 132 that concern us here only a few late ones (2 Baruch, 3 Baruch) bear the title in the MSS, and even there it may well be a scribal addition.

(3) Related to the last point is the fact that the Jewish apocalypses commonly embrace various distinct literary forms—visions, prayers, legends, etc. Hence the famous dictum of von Rad that "apocalyptic" is not a literary genre but a *mixtum compositum* (von Rad, 330). At this point Klaus Koch's distinction between complex and component types is helpful (Koch, 28). The undoubted diversity of the component literary types in the apocalypses cannot preclude the overarching consistency of a *Rahmengattung* or macrogenre.

The complexity of the apocalypses has two distinct aspects. First, literary forms are used in a subordinate way within a larger whole—e.g., prayers and exhortations within a vision. Second, many apocalypses juxtapose formally distinct units which are not clearly subordinate to each other (e.g., the visions in Daniel 7–12 and the *Similitudes of Enoch*) or string together a number of distinct units by means of a narrative framework (e.g., 4 Ezra, 2 Baruch). In the latter case some of the component units may be apocalypses in themselves. Such complexity is the norm rather than the exception, at least in the Jewish apocalypses. It cannot be adequately explained by source-critical theories. Even where independent sources are incorporated, we must still account for the composition of the final work. The complex apocalypse is a literary phenomenon in its own right.

1 Enoch presents a special problem in this regard. While the book as a whole might be considered a complex apocalypse, it is more commonly regarded as a collection of five independent works. We now know that the *Similitudes* were not part of the Enochic corpus at Qumran and that the *Astronomical Book* was copied separately (J. T. Milik, *The Books of Enoch* [Oxford: Oxford University Press, 1976]). It seems better, then, to treat *1 Enoch* as a collection of independent works, some of which are themselves complex apocalypses. (On the composition and unity of the various apocalypses see Collins, *Apocalyptic Imagination.*)

In recent years significant progress has been made toward a form-critical understanding of the apocalyptic literature. It will suffice here to note the work of Vielhauer, Koch, the Society of Biblical Literature group in *Semeia 14,* and most recently Hellholm. Vielhauer and Koch, in their valuable contributions, offered lists of typical features and constituent forms. The "morphology of the genre" in *Semeia 14* attempted a more systematic analysis by examining the distribution of the characteristic elements in the corpus of apocalyptic texts. In this way it was possible to arrive at a definition which stated the common core of the genre and to distinguish types and subgenres which are characterized by some of the elements, but not by others. In the process some attempt was made to distinguish different levels of abstraction (e.g., visual revelation might be in the form of visions or epiphanies; see Collins, ed., *Apocalypse*, 6). The purpose of *Semeia 14* was to delimit the macrogenre and provide a preliminary classification of the whole corpus of the genre. The classification was based on both form (manner of revelation) and content (the various types of eschatology). The analysis of constituent literary forms and subgenres was not pursued in any detail.

The most recent major study of the genre, by David Hellholm, relies on the methods of text linguistics rather than traditional form criticism. He characterizes his approach as "syntagmatic" in contrast to the "paradigmatic" approaches of Vielhauer, Koch, and *Semeia 14*. Hitherto he has published analyses of the *Shepherd of Hermas* and Revelation but has not completed his study of the genre at large. Consequently the final import of his work remains to be seen. Hellholm does not dispute the validity of the "paradigmatic" approach, but he makes some significant criticism of previous work. His main point concerns the need for greater differentiation among levels of abstraction and among criteria for classification which may be applied to a text. He has also called for greater attention to the function of the genre, a question which was deliberately bracketed in *Semeia 14*.

The distinction between different levels of abstraction bears directly on the definition of the genre. Hellholm ("Problem," 169) proposes the following hierarchy of generic concepts:

Mode of writing—Narrative
Type of text—Revelatory writing
Genre—Apocalypse
Subgenre—Apocalypse with otherworldly journey
Single text—*2 Enoch*, etc.

Several different levels can be discerned beyond the individual text. A particular literary form may be regarded as an independent genre or as a subtype of a broader category. The level of abstraction appropriate to the genre is determined in part by common usage and in part by the degree of coherence which we perceive within a group of texts. On one level, the works which are called apocalypses pertain to the category MYTH, in any of a number of senses, e.g., as a story about supernatural beings, or as a symbolic expression of basic intuitions, or as a narrative resolution of contradictory perceptions. Myth is a much broader category than apocalypse, however; thus the genre of these texts can be defined more helpfully on a lower level of abstraction.

In *Semeia 14* (p. 9) the genre was defined as follows: " '*Apocalypse' is a genre of revelatory literature with a narrative framework, in which a revelation is mediated by an otherworldly being to a human recipient, disclosing a transcendent reality which is both temporal, insofar as it envisages eschatological salvation, and spatial insofar as it involves another, supernatural world.*" This definition is based on a combination of form and content. It should be said at the outset that it is quite possible to define a genre on purely formal grounds, e.g., by ending the above definition after "a human recipient." To do so would simply move the definition to a higher level of generality and make it applicable to a wider range of texts (e.g., the visions of Zechariah would be included). On the other hand, the definition could be extended to address the questions of setting and function or intention. The definition given above, however, fits all the undisputed apocalypses and gives a more adequate description of them than the purely formal definition. It is our position that the recognition of this genre is not based on setting and function, but on the combination of form and content given above. The questions of setting and function are more complex than has generally been recognized and will be discussed separately below.

The two main types or subgenres distinguished in *Semeia 14* are apocalypses with and without an otherworldly journey. The point at issue here is not the presence or absence of a single motif. The OTHERWORLDLY JOURNEY provides the context for the revelation and determines the form of the work. All the Jewish apocalypses which have no otherworldly journey have a review of history in some form, and so they may be conveniently labeled "HISTORICAL" APOCALYPSES.

Before we proceed to the discussion of these two types we should note two features which apply to both.

First, the recipient of the revelation in the Jewish apocalypses is invariably a venerable ancient figure: Enoch, Daniel, Moses, Ezra, Baruch, Abraham. Usually the revelations are described, pseudonymously, by these figures, but they are recounted in the third person in *Jubilees* and in *Testament of Abraham*. The device of pseudonymity had some biblical precedent in Deuteronomy but was widespread in the Hellenistic world in material analogous to the apocalypses (e.g., the *Sibylline Oracles*, the Egyptian Potter's Oracle, the Persian Oracle of Hystaspes) as well as in other contexts. Its main function was undoubtedly to lend authority to the revelation. The pseudonyms were presumably chosen for their affinity with the subject matter. Enoch was the sage of heavenly mysteries par excellence; the halakhic material in *Jubilees* was ascribed to Moses.

Second, the narrative framework invariably contains some account of the way in which the revelation was received. We may distinguish between the *immediate* and *extended* frameworks. The immediate framework consists of an introduction and a conclusion. The introduction describes the circumstances attending the revelation and the disposition and reaction of the recipient. Prayer for revelation may be regarded as part of the opening frame (e.g., in Daniel 9, where the actual prayer seems to have been composed for a different context). The conclusion describes how the visionary awoke from sleep or was returned to earth. It may also contain the concluding instructions of the revealer and parenesis by the recipient to his children (e.g., in *2 Enoch*) or to a wider public (e.g., the concluding letter in *2 Baruch*). None of these features is invariable but there is always some immediate framework.

Several apocalypses have also an extended framework consisting of stories about the recipient (as in Daniel and *Apocalypse of Abraham*) or providing a larger context for the revelation (e.g., the *Book of the Watchers, 2 Baruch, Testament of Abraham*). This extended framework may be loosely structured and incorporate material that was originally independent (as in Daniel). It is not an essential part of the genre but it is by no means exceptional.

I. Basic Apocalyptic Genres

A. The "Historical" Apocalypses (Daniel; Book of Dreams and Apocalypse of Weeks in 1 Enoch; Jubilees; 4 Ezra; 2 Baruch)

1. The Media of Revelation

a. The Symbolic Dream Vision. The most common form of revelation in the "Historical" Apocalypses is the Symbolic Dream Vision, which is found in Daniel 7–8; *1 Enoch* 83–84; 85–91; 4 Ezra 11–12; 13; *2 Baruch* 35–47; 53–77. The usual pattern of these visions is:

(1) Indication of the circumstances.
(2) Description of the vision, introduced by a term such as "behold."
(3) Request for interpretation, often because of fear. The request takes the form of lengthy prayers in *2 Baruch*.
(4) Interpretation by an angel. (God interprets the vision in *2 Baruch* 39.)
(5) Concluding material is variable. It may include the reaction of the seer, instructions of the angel, and Parenesis (in *2 Baruch* and 4 Ezra 12).

The symbolic dream vision, then, can be a formally complete apocalypse in itself, but in the Jewish corpus it is always combined with other literary forms in a complex apocalypse (unless the *Animal Apocalypse* in *1 Enoch* 85–91 is considered apart from the *Book of Dreams* [*1 Enoch* 83–84]). The dream visions of Enoch are exceptional in that there is no request and subsequent interpretation. In *1 Enoch* 83–84 Enoch's grandfather Malalel inquires about the dream and volunteers an interpretation which moves Enoch to pray for mercy. This vision in itself lacks the angelic mediation and is not an apocalypse. In the *Animal Apocalypse* (*1 Enoch* 85–91) there is no interpretation, but the vision is still mediated by three angels who lift Enoch up from the earth onto a high place (87:3). This episode does not amount to an otherworldly journey, but the role of the angels is closer to that of tour guide than interpreter.

The symbolism of these visions is usually allegorical, i.e., the object seen stands for something else: four beasts represent four kings, a lion and an eagle represent the messiah and Rome. In some cases, however, the symbols are mythic-realistic. In 4 Ezra the man from the sea is identified rather than interpreted. Similarly, in Daniel 7 the divine throne does not stand for something else but has its own reality. Both allegorical and mythic-realistic symbols can be found in a single vision (e.g., Daniel 7).

The dream visions in the apocalypses can be viewed as a late development in the history of a symbolic vision form beginning with Amos (Niditch; Koch,

"Visionsbericht"). If we juxtapose the two ends of the spectrum, however, we find that their forms are quite different. In Amos 7:7-9; 8:1-3 there is no narrative frame describing the circumstances of the revelation. The vision is not a dream, and is very simple; it is a matter of perceiving symbolic significance in a commonplace object (the plumbline, the basket of fruit). Amos does not ask for an interpretation. Instead God asks him what he sees and provides an interpretation. God, not an angel, is the prophet's partner in dialogue. The claim that the visions of Daniel and 4 Ezra are nonetheless part of a tradition which goes back to Amos rests mainly on the mediating form of the visions of Zechariah. The first vision of Zechariah (1:7-17) is introduced by "I saw in the night," therefore presumably in a dream. Again in 4:1 an angel "waked me, like a man that is wakened out of his sleep." The dream context may also be implied in the other visions. Here the dialogue partner is an angel. In Zech 5:1-4 the angel asks Zechariah what he sees and then provides an interpretation, after the manner of the visions of Amos. In Zech 1:7-17; 2:1-4 (*RSV* 1:18-21); and 6:1-8 only the seer asks questions. In these cases we are closer to the form of the apocalyptic dream vision.

The dream visions in the apocalypses can also be viewed as an adaptation of the symbolic dreams which are attested throughout the Near East. According to A. Leo Oppenheim (p. 187):

> The typical dream-report of our source-material appears within a strictly conventionalized "frame," the pattern of which can be reconstructed from evidence that is surprisingly uniform from the Sumer of the third millennium up to Ptolemaic Egypt and from Mesopotamia westward to Greece. . . . The "frame" . . . consists of an introduction which tells about the dreamer, the locality and other circumstances of the dream which were considered of import. The actual report of the dream-content follows and is succeeded by the final part of the "frame" which describes the end of the dream and often includes a section referring to the reaction of the dreaming person, or, also, to the actual fulfillment of the prediction or promise contained in the dream.

The visions of Amos have no such frame. Zechariah provides a date for the first vision (1:7) but no other circumstances. By contrast the "frame" is characteristic of the apocalyptic dream visions. The lengthy descriptions of the visions in Daniel and the apocalypses are also closer to the conventions of dream reports than to the symbolic visions of the prophets.

While dreams were widely attested in the early books of the Bible, *symbolic* dreams were often viewed with distrust (Deut 13:2-6 [*RSV* 1-5]; Jer 23:25-32; 27:9-10; 29:8-9; Sir 31[34]:1-8). The main biblical reports of symbolic dreams are in the stories of Joseph and Daniel, both of whom serve a Gentile king in a foreign land. (Joseph's own dreams are prior to his exile, and there is a very brief report of a symbolic dream in an Israelite context in Judg 7:13-14.) In view of the Babylonian setting of Daniel 1-6 and of the Babylonian associations of *Enoch* (VanderKam), it seems likely that the postexilic development of the Jewish visionary tradition was influenced by contact with the mantic wisdom of the Babylonians. This is not to say that the apocalyptic dream vision was a foreign borrowing, but that it combined elements from different sources in a new form.

One major element in the apocalyptic visions is the role of the interpreting

7

angel. This element is found already in Zechariah. We might also compare Ezekiel's angelic guide in Ezekiel 40–48. The introduction of this figure is an innovation over against the preexilic biblical tradition and also over against usual dream interpretation. There are some Near Eastern precedents for supernatural dream interpreters, e.g., in the dream of Gudea which is interpreted by the goddess Nanshe (Oppenheim, 245-46).

An intriguing parallel to the apocalypses is found in the Persian Bahman Yasht, where Zarathustra sees a symbolic vision of a tree with four branches. (So ch. 1; a variant in ch. 3 has a dream vision of a tree with seven branches.) Ahura Mazda interprets the branches as periods which are to come. The Yasht in its present form is a late composition from the Christian era, but it is widely believed to preserve early material from the Avesta. Unlike the Babylonian material, the Yasht resembles the Jewish apocalypses in both form and content. Persian influence was of course possible, even in Zechariah, but the notorious difficulty of dating the Persian material makes the discussion inconclusive.

Much remains unclear in the history of the symbolic vision. There was certainly continuity with the biblical tradition, but we must also allow for influence from Near Eastern dream interpretation and possibly from Persian sources too. In any case the apocalyptic writers display considerable creativity.

Within the apocalyptic corpus, the influence of Daniel is evident in *2 Baruch* 35–47 and in 4 Ezra 11–13. Yet we can not ascribe all apocalyptic visions to a single stream. The dream visions of *1 Enoch* are independent of (and possibly older than) those of Daniel, and the vision of the cloud and waters in *2 Baruch* is not related to Danielic tradition either. The vision form undergoes some development in the book of Revelation, where the dream setting is abandoned. Instead these visions are ecstatic, occurring in a waking state. The symbolism is sometimes interpreted allegorically (e.g., ch. 17) but is often mythic-realistic. In the Jewish apocalypses ecstatic waking revelation is associated with epiphanies and some otherworldly journeys rather than with symbolic visions. The book of Revelation includes a rapture of John to heaven in ch. 4 and adapts some of the characteristics of the heavenly journey, although most of the visions seem to be set on earth.

b. Epiphany. An EPIPHANY is a vision of a single supernatural figure, such as the angel in Daniel 10. It is less comprehensive in form than the dream vision and cannot constitute an apocalypse without supplementary forms. The epiphany in Daniel 10 takes the place of the description of the dream vision and is accompanied by an indication of the circumstances and of the visionary's reaction. It is followed not by an interpretation but by an angelic discourse which gives the content of the revelation.

Important precedents for the apocalyptic epiphany are found in Ezekiel, in the theophany in chs. 1–2 and in the angelic epiphany in ch. 8. More broadly, the epiphany followed by a revelation is a modification of the common pattern of "message dreams" (as opposed to "symbolic dreams"). According to Oppenheim (p. 191): "In the Near East . . . the theophany is the prototype of the message dream. The deity appears and addresses the sleeping person for whom submissive consent is the only admissible reaction."

In the early books of the OT we often read that "God came to X in a dream by night . . ." (e.g., Gen 20:3; 31:24; 1 Kgs 3:5; 9:2) but the apparition is not described. Divine dream figures are sometimes described in dream reports from the ancient Near East. In the dream of Gudea: "In the dream, the first man—like the heaven was his surpassing (size), like the earth was his surpassing (size), (according) to his (horn-crowned (?)) head he was a god, (according) to his wings he was Imdugud (the bird of the Weather-god), (according) to his lower parts (?) he was the Storm-flood, lions were lying to his right and left—commanded me to build his house . . ." (Oppenheim, 245). In the fragmentary Dream of Merneptah "his majesty saw in a dream as if it were the image of Ptah standing in the presence of the Pharaoh, (and) he was as high as . . ." (Oppenheim, 251). Dream theophanies are also common in later classical sources.

An exceptional fusion of epiphany and symbolic vision is found in 4 Ezra 9:26–10:59. Ezra sees a woman and enters into dialogue with her. "While I was talking to her, behold, her face suddenly shone exceedingly, and her countenance flashed like lightning, so that I was too frightened to approach her" (10:25). The woman is transformed into "an established city." The angel Uriel then comes and explains that this woman/city is Zion.

c. Angelic Discourse. An ANGELIC DISCOURSE is a revelation delivered as a speech by an angel. It may follow an epiphany as in Daniel 10–11 or be reported without visual elements as in *Jub.* 2:1ff. *Jubilees* is exceptional among the apocalyptic writings in that it has neither vision nor epiphany, and its status as an apocalypse is often questioned. It is in fact a mixed form, since it is simultaneously an angelic revelation and a midrash on Genesis.

The angelic discourse, like the epiphany, has its most plausible background in the "message dreams" of the ancient Near East.

d. Revelatory Dialogue. A REVELATORY DIALOGUE is a conversation between the recipient and the revealer (either God or an angel). It is distinguished from other dialogue by the supernatural dialogue partner. There is usually some dialogue in the symbolic visions, but dialogue is also used independently, side by side with visions, in 4 Ezra and *2 Baruch.*

Dialogue is rare in dream reports (Oppenheim, 191). The supplementary use of dialogue in vision reports has a long history in the prophetic visions. The independent use of dialogue in 4 Ezra and *2 Baruch* bears some analogy to the dialogues of Job or the Babylonian Theodicy, but the relationship between the dialogue partners is very different in the apocalyptic context since one of them is an angel.

Revelatory dialogue and discourse figure more prominently in later Gnostic apocalypses than in the Jewish corpus. (See F. T. Fallon, "The Gnostic Apocalypses," in *Semeia 14: Apocalypse: The Morphology of a Genre* [ed. J. J. Collins; Missoula: Scholars Press, 1979] 123-58.)

e. Midrash. A MIDRASH is "a work that attempts to make a text of Scripture understandable, useful, and relevant for a later generation. It is the text of Scripture which is the point of departure, and it is for the sake of the text that the midrash exists" (Wright, 74). Different kinds of midrash can be distinguished: homiletic, exegetical, or narrative. The clearest example of an exegetical midrash in an apocalypse is in Daniel 9, where the angel Gabriel provides an explanation of the seventy weeks of Jeremiah. The book of *Jubilees* may be viewed as a narrative midrash on Genesis. Both Daniel 9 and *Jubilees* present the midrash as an angelic discourse.

The term midrash is often applied loosely to apocalyptic texts because they are studded with biblical allusions. A midrash, however, takes its point of departure from the biblical text. Even in 4 Ezra 12:11, where the eagle is identified with the fourth kingdom of Daniel, the biblical text is not the point of departure and the designation midrash is not appropriate.

f. Pesher. PESHER is closely related to exegetical midrash. The term is used for the interpretation of dreams and of the writing on the wall in Daniel and for the biblical commentaries at Qumran. The commentary is direct and explicit and treats the text or dream piecemeal. The Qumran *pesharim* have their own literary structure. They proceed systematically from one textual unit to another and introduce the pesher by formulas. The apocalypses contain no example of a developed pesher in the Qumran sense. Daniel 9 is the only passage which comes into consideration. Since only one biblical phrase is interpreted there, the parallel with Qumran is limited, but there is an analogy in the style of interpretation. If we regard exegetical midrash and pesher as overlapping terms, either might be appropriate for Daniel 9. By contrast, *Jubilees* is not a pesher since it does not cite the biblical text and comment on it piece by piece.

The origin of the pesher genre is clearly related to dream interpretation. The cognate Akkadian verb *pašāru* was used for (1) reporting the dream to another person, (2) the interpretation by discerning the message of the deity, and (3) the process of dispelling the evil consequences of a dream. While the term pesher in Daniel and in the Qumran texts has lost some of these connotations and modified others, there is obvious continuity with dream interpretation. In the interpretation of the dream of Tammuz (Oppenheim, 246) the individual units of the dream are repeated and then followed by their interpretation:

> "A single reed was shaking its head for you (this means):
> your mother who bore you will shake her head for you.
> Two several reeds—one was removed for you (this means):
> I and you, one (of us) will be removed. . . ."

(Cf. the interpretation of the dream in Daniel 2 and of the apocalyptic dream vision in 4 Ezra 12.)

This style of interpretation of a revelatory text is attested outside Judaism in the Hellenistic age in the Egyptian Demotic Chronicle. This document also bears some analogy to the content of the "historical" apocalypses since it contains predictions of oppression and prophesies the restoration of Egypt under a native king (F. Daumas, "Littérature prophétique et exégétique Égyptienne et commentaires Esséniens," *A la rencontre de Dieu. Mémorial A. Gelin* [Le Puy: X. Mappus, 1961] 203-21).

g. Revelation Report. The *Apocalypse of Weeks* in *1 Enoch* 93:1-10; 91:12-19 is cast as a speech of Enoch to his children "according to that which appeared to me in the heavenly vision, and (which) I know from the words of the holy angels and understand from the tablets of heaven." The heavenly vision is not described but the content of the revelation is reported. The media of revelation presupposed here include at least epiphany and angelic discourse. The "heavenly vision" and the reference to the tablets of heaven could be taken to imply the ascent of Enoch, but there is no explicit reference to an otherworldly journey.

The speech of Enoch here is not a TESTAMENT, since it is not a farewell discourse or deathbed scene.

2. The Content of the Revelation

The content of the "historical" apocalypses has its own typical forms. There can be no attempt here to catalog every literary form that occurs in an apocalypse, but only to discuss those which are characteristic of the genre.

a. Ex Eventu Prophecy. EX EVENTU PROPHECY, the prediction of events which have already taken place, is found in all the Jewish apocalypses which do not have otherworldly journeys (not necessarily in all units of these apocalypses): Daniel 7, 8, 9, 10–11; *Animal Apocalypse, Apocalypse of Weeks; Jub.* 23:11-26; *4 Ezra* 11–12; *2 Baruch* 35–47; 53–77. The only *ex eventu* prophecy in the context of an otherworldly journey in the Jewish apocalypses is found in *Apocalypse of Abraham.*

Ex eventu prophecy is an old phenomenon in the Bible; an early example can be found in Gen 15:13-16. The apocalyptic use of the form always leads to an eschatological conclusion. (This is also often true of oracles and testaments in the Hellenistic period.) In *Jubilees* 23 the prophecy is relatively unstructured. Elsewhere the apocalyptic *ex eventu* prophecies fall into two types: periodization of history and regnal prophecy.

(1) Periodization of History. The PERIODIZATION OF HISTORY is the division of history, or a significant segment of it, into a set number of periods; it is the most characteristic form of *ex eventu* prophecy in the apocalypses. The number of periods may vary: four kingdoms (Daniel 7; *2 Baruch* 36–39; cf. 4 Ezra 12:11), seventy weeks of years (Daniel 9), seventy shepherds *(Animal Apocalypse),* ten weeks *(Apocalypse of Weeks:* seven before the turning point of history), twelve periods (plus two unnumbered periods, *2 Baruch* 56–72). Periodization is also widely used in the *Sibylline Oracles,* especially in *Sibylline Oracles* 1–2 and *Sibylline Oracles* 4, and is attested in the Qumran Scrolls (11QMelchizedek, the Pesher on the Periods). This kind of schematization has no real precedent in the OT. The four-kingdom schema was widely known in the Hellenistic period and is attested in the Roman author Aemilius Sura, and, very differently, in the Persian Bahman Yasht. The tenfold division of history was implied in Virgil's fourth eclogue according to the commentary of Servius. The declining ages of humanity were already numbered in Hesiod's *Works and Days.* The ultimate source of the phenomenon of periodization should be sought in Persian thought. Persian parallels can be found for divisions of history into four, seven, ten (all in the Bahman Yasht) and twelve (Bundahishn) periods. (See further Flusser.)

The division of history into a set number of periods served two purposes in the apocalypses. First, it enhanced the deterministic sense that history was measured out and under control. Second, it enabled the reader to locate his own generation near the end of the sequence. In the latter sense the periodized prophecy could serve as an "apocalyptic timetable" (Hartman) without attempting to specify the date of the eschaton.

(2) Regnal Prophecy. Some *ex eventu* prophecies, such as Daniel 11, do not divide history into a set number of periods, but "predict" the ongoing rise and fall of kings and kingdoms (hence the term REGNAL PROPHECY). Light has been shed on this literary form by the publication of Akkadian prophecies. The genre has been described by A. K. Grayson (p. 13) as follows: "they consist in the main of predictions after the event *(vaticinia ex eventu).* The predictions are divided according to reigns and often begin with some such phrase as 'a prince will arise.' Although the kings are never named it is sometimes possible to identify them on the basis of details provided in the 'prophetic' description. The reigns are characterized as 'good' or 'bad' and the phraseology is borrowed from omen literature." The last point, concerning the characterization of the reigns, does not hold for the Jewish adaptations of the genre. A major Babylonian example from the Hellenistic period is found in the so-called Dynastic Prophecy (Grayson, 24-37). The main apocalyptic examples are found in Daniel 11 and 8:23-27. Similar material is found in the *Sibylline Oracles* (e.g., *Sib. Or.* 5:1-51). Features of regnal prophecy may also be combined with periodization, e.g., in Daniel 7 and 4 Ezra 12.

The purpose of the *ex eventu* regnal prophecies is not very different from that of the periodizations. Again the sense is conveyed that history is predetermined and has nearly run its course.

b. Eschatological Predictions. All the "historical" apocalypses have ESCHATOLOGICAL PREDICTIONS, which invariably fall into a pattern of crisis-judgment-salvation (see Collins, ed., *Apocalypse,* 28). It is characteristic of these writings that the judgment and salvation include the restoration of the Jewish people, but also transcend the bounds of ordinary history by the cosmic scope of the judgment and by provision of retribution for the dead, usually through resurrection. (In *Jub.* 23:31 the spirits of the righteous will have much joy.) In many cases the details of the eschatological scenario are simply stated. In a few cases we can discern literary forms. The most important of these are the following:

(1) The Signs of the End. The *ex eventu* prophecies often conclude with a crisis (e.g., the allusions to the persecution in Daniel 7, 8, and 11 or the perverse seventh week in *Apocalypse of Weeks*). Some also include a more general reference to eschatological upheavals, e.g., Dan 12:1: "And there shall be a time of trouble, such as never has been since there was a nation till that time." In 4 Ezra and *2 Baruch,* however, there is a developed form of eschatological woes which are SIGNS OF THE END: 4 Ezra 5:1-13; 6:8-28; 13:30-31; *2 Baruch* 27; 70. (Cf. *1 Enoch* 80.) The signs are characterized by cosmic disturbances as well as by the disruption of human affairs. The form is familiar from the Synoptic Gospels: "But in those days, after that tribulation, the sun will be darkened and the moon will not give its light, and the stars will be falling from heaven, and the powers in the heavens will be shaken" (Mark 13:24-25; cf. Matt 24:4-36; Luke 21:8-36).

The antecedents of this form can be found in OT prophecy, e.g., Joel 3:1-2 (*RSV* 2:30-31): "And I will give portents in the heavens and on the earth, blood and fire and columns of smoke. The sun shall be turned to darkness, and the moon to blood, before the great and terrible day of the Lord comes." More generally compare Isaiah 24 (v. 3: "The earth shall be utterly laid waste . . ."), where an affinity with old fertility myths is apparent. Portents and omens (e.g.,

Jub. 23:25: "the heads of children shall be white with grey hair") were a subject of great interest in ancient Babylonia. They are also common in Greco-Roman literature (see already Hesiod *Works and Days* 181 for the sign of children with grey hair). They are well attested in the *Sibylline Oracles,* where they sometimes have eschatological significance and sometimes not. An overview of the signs in Jewish and Christian material with Greco-Roman parallels can be found in K. Berger, "Hellenistisch-heidnische Prodigien und die Vorzeichen jüdischer und christlicher Apokalyptik," *ANRW* II.23.2 (1980) 1428-69.

The function of these signs is to evoke an awesome fear and to serve as a foil for the eschatological salvation which is to follow.

(2) Description of Judgment Scene. Some indication of a coming judgment is found in all the apocalypses, but more elaborate DESCRIPTIONS OF JUDGMENT SCENES are found in Dan 7:9-14; *1 Enoch* 90:20-38 (the *Animal Apocalypse*); and 4 Ezra 7:33-38. The basic features of these scenes are the enthronement of the heavenly judge and the execution of the judgment. Daniel and the *Animal Apocalypse* also share the motif of the opening of the books. In 4 Ezra 7 God addresses the condemned so that they recognize their error. This motif of recognition is attested in judgment scenes in the *Similitudes of Enoch* (*1 Enoch* 62) and the Wisdom of Solomon 5. Cf. also *2 Bar.* 51:4-6. The divine address to the condemned is paralleled in the judgment scene in Matt 25:31-46.

The judgment scenes in the "historical" apocalypses are concerned with whole peoples rather than with individuals. There is no close biblical parallel for the descriptions of the judgment which we find in Daniel and *1 Enoch.* Yet the tradition that Yahweh is judge of the earth and will come to judge the world is associated with the kingship of Yahweh in the Psalms (e.g., 96:10; 98:6-9). In Psalm 82 Yahweh presides as judge over the other gods in the divine council. This psalm presupposes a more elaborate mythology than is explicit in the Bible. The roots of the tradition are presumably Canaanite, although there is little documentation. (See, however, *Ugaritica* V, text 2, where El is enthroned as judge.) Neither the Canaanite nor Israelite traditions (prior to the apocalypses) envisaged a judgment of the dead. Even the judgment scene in Daniel 7 is not explicitly concerned with the dead, although a judgment of resurrected individuals is clearly envisaged in ch. 12. By contrast, the judgment scene in 4 Ezra 7 is explicitly set after the resurrection (cf. the judgment scene in Revelation 20).

(3) Epiphany of a Heavenly Figure. Apart from the epiphany of the revealer figure, we also find an EPIPHANY of a heavenly figure within the vision in Dan 7:13-14 and in 4 Ezra 13. While the passage in 4 Ezra is clearly dependent on Daniel, the setting is different. In Daniel the figure on the clouds receives judgment; in 4 Ezra he executes judgment. We should note that while a number of apocalypses *announce* the advent of a savior figure (Michael in Dan 12:1; the messiah in 4 Ezra 7:28; 12:32; *2 Bar.* 29:3; 39:7; 72:2 *Apoc. Ab.* 31:1), descriptions of an epiphany are rare. In the *Animal Apocalypse* God himself (the Lord of the Sheep) is said to come down (*1 Enoch* 90:14, 18).

These epiphanies are clearly related to the theophany tradition in the OT (J. Jeremias), which in turn has its roots in Canaanite myth (F. M. Cross, *Canaanite Myth and Hebrew Epic* [Cambridge, Mass.: Harvard University Press, 1973] 147-94). A full-blown THEOPHANY is found in *1 Enoch* 1. (See J. VanderKam, "The Theophany of Enoch I 3b-7, 9," *VT* 23 [1973] 129-50.)

(4) Prophecy of Cosmic Transformation. Cosmic transformation is a standard fea-

ture of the "historical" apocalypses, but only rarely do we find an extended PROPHECY OF COSMIC TRANSFORMATION: *Jub.* 23:27-31; *2 Baruch* 73-74 (cf. also the description of the day of judgment in 4 Ezra 7:39-43). These prophecies have their roots in the utopian oracles of the OT, e.g., Isa 11:1-9; 65:17-25.

Bibliography

G. Brooke, "Qumran Pesher: Towards the Redefinition of a Genre," *RevQ* 10 (1979/81) 483-503; W. H. Brownlee, *The Midrash Pesher of Habakkuk* (SBLMS 24; Missoula: Scholars Press, 1979); J. J. Collins, "Pseudonymity, Historical Reviews and the Genre of the Revelation of John," *CBQ* 39 (1977) 329-43; E. L. Ehrlich, *Der Traum im Alten Testament* (BZAW 73; Berlin: Töpelmann, 1953); M. Fishbane, "The Qumran Pesher and Traits of Ancient Hermeneutics," in *Proceedings of the Sixth World Congress of Jewish Studies* (Jerusalem: World Union of Jewish Studies, 1977) 97-114; D. Flusser, "The four empires in the Fourth Sibyl and in the Book of Daniel," *Israel Oriental Studies* 2 (1972) 148-75; A. K. Grayson, *Babylonian Historical-Literary Texts* (Toronto: University of Toronto Press, 1975); J. S. Hanson, "Dreams and Visions in the Graeco-Roman World and Early Christianity," *ANRW* II.23.2 (1980) 1395-1427; L. Hartman, "The Function of Some So-Called Apocalyptic Timetables," *NTS* 22 (1976) 1-14; idem, *Prophecy Interpreted* (ConB 1; Lund: Gleerup, 1966); M. Hengel, *Judaism and Hellenism* (tr. J. Bowden; Philadelphia: Fortress, 1974) 1.175-210; M. P. Horgan, *Pesharim: Qumran Interpretations of Biblical Books* (CBQMS 8; Washington: Catholic Biblical Association of America, 1979); A. Hultgård, "Forms and Origin of Iranian Apocalyptics," in *Apocalypticism in the Mediterranean World and the Near East* (ed. D. Hellholm; Tübingen: Mohr, 1983) 387-411; C. Jeremias, *Die Nachtgesichte des Sacharja* (FRLANT 117; Göttingen: Vandenhoeck & Ruprecht, 1977); Jörg Jeremias, *Theophanie: Die Geschichte einer alttestamentlichen Gattung* (WMANT 10; Neukirchen-Vluyn: Neukirchener, 1965); R. Kearns, *Vorfragen zur Christologie. II: Überlieferungsgeschichtliche und Rezeptionsgeschichtliche Studien zur Vorgeschichte eines christologischen Hoheitstitels* (Tübingen: Mohr, 1980) 8-15; K. Koch, "Vom profetischen zum apokalyptischen Visionsbericht," in *Apocalypticism in the Mediterranean World and the Near East* (ed. D. Hellholm; Tübingen: Mohr, 1983) 413-46; W. G. Lambert, *The Background of Jewish Apocalyptic* (London: Athlone Press, 1978); G. W. Nickelsburg, *Resurrection, Immortality, and Eternal Life in Intertestamental Judaism* (HTS 26; Cambridge, Mass.: Harvard University Press, 1972); S. Niditch, *The Symbolic Vision in Biblical Tradition* (HSM 30; Chico: Scholars Press, 1983); A. L. Oppenheim, *The Interpretation of Dreams in the Ancient Near East* (Philadelphia: American Philosophical Society, 1956); S. B. Reid, "The Sociological Setting of the Historical Apocalypses of I Enoch and the Book of Daniel" (Diss., Emory University, 1981); W. Richter, "Traum und Traumdeutung im AT: Ihre Form und Verwendung," *BZ* 7 (1963) 202-20; J. VanderKam, *Enoch and the Growth of an Apocalyptic Tradition* (CBQMS 16; Washington: Catholic Biblical Association of America, 1984); A. G. Wright, *The Literary Genre Midrash* (Staten Island: Alba House, 1965).

B. Otherworldly Journeys (Book of the Watchers, Astronomical Book, Similitudes [all in 1 Enoch]; 2 Enoch; 3 Baruch; Testament of Abraham; Apocalypse of Abraham; Apocalypse of Zephaniah; Testament of Levi 2 – 5)

The OTHERWORLDLY JOURNEY is a subgenre of apocalypse rather than an independent genre, and its component forms often overlap with those of the "historical" apocalypses. The otherworldly journeys are visionary experiences and are mediated by angels who serve as guides and interpreters. While the symbolic dream vision was primarily allegorical, the mode of the journey apocalypses is predominantly mythic-realistic, i.e., the heavens and their contents are not understood as allegories for something else. Of course, the contrast is not absolute. We have seen that the dream visions include some mythic-realistic material, and occasional items in the journey apocalypses can be interpreted allegorically.

Here again there are connections with ancient Near Eastern dream reports. The revelation is presented within a narrative frame that describes the circumstances in which the revelation occurred, the ascent (or descent) of the visionary, and his return to his place at the end. (The full frame is not found in all cases.) In two of the oldest apocalypses, *1 Enoch* 13–14 and *Testament of Levi* 2, the revelation is explicitly said to occur in a dream, and in *2 Enoch* the visionary is awakened from sleep for the ascent. Dream travels to the netherworld are attested as early as the death dream of Enkidu in the Gilgamesh Epic (Oppenheim, 213, 248-49). The Assyrian dream book provides a commentary on dream travels to both heaven and the netherworld (Oppenheim, 267, 281-83). This commentary proposes interpretations for various elements in dream travels (e.g., "If he hears in heaven repeatedly rumors of accusations: he will have worries . . .") but do not describe actual dreams. A report of an Assyrian dream vision of the netherworld can be found in *ANET*, 109-10.

Ascents and descents are also widely attested outside of dream reports. In the Babylonian area, the ascents of Enmeduranki, the seventh king, and Utuabzu, the seventh sage, have been invoked as models for *Enoch* (see VanderKam). Descents to the netherworld were ascribed to the Sumerian goddess Inanna and the Babylonian goddess Ishtar. In the Greco-Roman world there is a tradition of heavenly journeys in philosophical texts in which Plato's *Myth of Er* played a formative role (other examples include Cicero's *Somnium Scipionis*, Seneca's *Ad Marciam de consolatione* 26, Plutarch's *De genio Socratis* 21-22 [the Oracle of Trophonius], and *De sera numinis vindicta* 22-31). The genre is parodied in Lucian's *Icaromenippus*. Descents to the underworld are found in Homer *Odyssey* 11 and Virgil *Aeneid* 6 and are parodied in Lucian's *Kataplous* and *Nekyomanteia*. (For an overview see Attridge; more detailed discussion in Betz.) The motifs of ascent and descent were already parodied by Aristophanes in the *Peace* and *Frogs* respectively. The best Persian illustration of an ascent is found in the Book of Arda Viraf, which is a full-blown apocalypse. This book is late (9th century) in its present form, but the motif of ascent is old in Persian tradition (cf. Vendidad 19:90-111; see Bousset, 155-228).

Biblical tradition by contrast has no clear precedent for the apocalyptic otherworldly journey. The OT does not describe what Enoch or Elijah saw when they were taken up. The prophets are said to stand in the divine council (Jer 23:18; cf. 1 Kings 22) but in no case is their ascent described. The nearest biblical approximation to this type of apocalypse is found in Ezekiel's guided tour of the temple area in Ezekiel 40–48, but this involves neither an ascent to heaven nor a descent to the netherworld.

For subsequent Christian and Gnostic use of the genre, see A. Yarbro Collins, "The Early Christian Apocalypses," in *Semeia 14: Apocalypse: The Morphology of a Genre* (ed. J. J. Collins; Missoula: Scholars Press, 1979) 61-121; F. T. Fallon, "The Gnostic Apocalypses," *ibid.*, 123-58.

1. The Media of Revelation

a. Transportation of the Visionary.

(1) Report of Ascent. In all the Jewish apocalypses of the journey type the visionary ascends to heaven. The means of ascent varies: clouds (*1 Enoch* 14; 39), the wings of angels (*2 Enoch* 3:1), the wing of a bird *(Apocalypse of Abraham)*, a chariot *(Testament of Abraham)*. In the *Astronomical Book* in *1 Enoch* 72–82 the ascent is not described, but the revelations presuppose the framework of a journey in which Enoch is guided by Uriel (74:2). *1 Enoch* 81:5 describes how seven holy ones brought Enoch back to earth before the door of his house.

(2) Report of Descent. No description of a descent has survived in a Jewish work, but *Apocalypse of Zephaniah* contains visions of the netherworld and presupposes a descent. In *1 Enoch* 22 Enoch journeys to the abodes of the dead inside a mountain.

b. The Revelation Account. Two subtypes may be distinguished:

(1) Report of a Tour. The *Book of the Watchers* has Enoch range to the ends of the earth. In the *Astronomical Book* Enoch is also taken to the ends of the earth (76:1) but his tour is mainly concerned with the heavenly bodies. The *Similitudes of Enoch* also use the tour format, although the movements of Enoch receive little attention (see, e.g., 52:1). In *Testament of Abraham* Abraham is given a chariot ride over the earth before he is taken to the first gate of heaven. These tours are quite diverse and are distinguished by their lack of a consistent organizing principle.

(2) Report of Ascent through a Numbered Series of Heavens. This continued ascent is distinguished from the initial elevation since it provides a way of structuring the content of the revelation. The numbered ascent makes for a much tighter and more consistent literary form than the relatively unstructured tour.

While the OT distinguishes "heaven" and "the heaven of heavens" (e.g., 1 Kgs 8:27), the apocalyptic distinction of multiple heavens first appears in the Hellenistic period, and is most probably due to Babylonian influence (see the discussions of Bousset, Morfill and Charles, and Bietenhard). The oldest Jewish apocalypse of this type, *Testament of Levi* 2–5, originally envisaged only three heavens, but the number was subsequently increased to seven. The original number would seem to accord with Paul's rapture to the third heaven in 2 Cor 12:2. *3 Baruch* describes five heavens but the throne of God is still above them. Origen *De Prin.* 2.3.6 refers to a book of Baruch in connection with seven heavens, and so may have known this book in a different form. Otherwise the standard number of heavens is seven: *2 Enoch, Apocalypse of Abraham, Ascension of Isaiah* (Christian, but probably with a Jewish substratum), and in rabbinic tradition (e.g., *b. Hag.* 12b).

The distinction of seven heavens is usually thought to be related to the Babylonian observation of the seven planets (e.g., Bietenhard, 15; Morfill and Charles, xxxii). The conception is more clearly attested in Persian religion, although the evidence is late. The clearest formulation is in the Book of Arda Viraf. According to Celsus the mysteries of Mithra conceived of a ladder of seven steps made of seven different metals that symbolized the ascent of the soul after death (Origen *Contra Celsum* 6.22).

The numbered sequence of heavens functions in the apocalypses in a manner analogous to the numbered periods of history. It demonstrates the order that pervades creation even though that order may be obscured by a crisis on earth.

Within the context of both the tours and the ascents revelation is predominantly in the form of visions. These are mythic-realistic rather than allegorical and are introduced simply by "I saw," without an introductory formula such as "behold." Dialogue with the angelic guide plays a subsidiary role. Discourse by God himself plays a significant role in *2 Enoch* 24–36. Cf. also God's address to Enoch in *1 Enoch* 15–16.

2. The Content of the Revelation

The subjects discussed in these apocalypses are fairly constant. They include cosmological matters relating to the sun, stars, and natural phenomena, the abodes of the dead in the places of reward and punishment, the angels, and often the throne of God. In some cases these materials are sufficiently stereotyped in expression that we can speak of literary forms. The *ex eventu* prophecies, which are so characteristic of the "historical" apocalypses, are found only in *Apocalypse of Abraham* of the journey type. There history is divided into twelve periods and the judgment is preceded by ten plagues. The main forms in this type of apocalypse are:

a. *Lists of Revealed Things.* Summary LISTS OF REVEALED THINGS are found in *1 Enoch* 41:1-7; 43:1-2; 60:11-22; *2 Enoch* 23:1; 40:1-13. These lists are primarily concerned with cosmological secrets: "all things in heaven and earth and sea, the courses and dwellings of all the elements, the seasons of the years, the courses and mutations of the days and the commandments and teachings" (*2 Enoch* 23:1). They can also include matters of eschatological interest such as "the dwelling of the chosen and the resting-places of the holy" (*1 Enoch* 41:2). Similar lists are given as the content of the revelation to Moses on Mount Sinai in *2 Bar.* 59:5-11 and Pseudo-Philo's *Liber Antiquitatum Biblicarum* 19:10. They are reflected negatively in 4 Ezra 4 and 5 in the impossible questions posed to Ezra by the angel: "Come, weigh me the weight of fire or measure me the measure of wind. . . ." These lists have been related to the wisdom tradition as exemplified in Job 38 and to the hymns to God as creator in the Psalms (Stone).

b. *Visions of the Abodes of the Dead.* Descriptions of heaven and hell become quite common in later Christian apocalypses. The only Jewish apocalypse which may be said to contain DESCRIPTIONS OF THE ABODES OF THE DEAD in a stereotyped form is *Apocalypse of Zephaniah.* Less developed visions of the abodes of the dead are found in *1 Enoch* 22; *2 Enoch* 8–10; *1 Enoch* 39:4-8 *(Similitudes)*; *3 Baruch* 3 and 10. In *1 Enoch* 22 these places are located inside a mountain in accordance with Babylonian tradition. In the *Similitudes* the abode of the righteous is at the end of heaven. In *2 Enoch* and *3 Baruch* the places of both righteous and wicked are in the heavens. In *2 Enoch* the place prepared for the righteous is Paradise. There is also a vision of Paradise in *1 Enoch* 32:3-6, but the description of these places had not yet become stereotyped in the Jewish apocalypses.

Visions of the netherworld as the abode of the dead are attested as far back as the Gilgamesh Epic and *Odyssey* Book 11. The differentiation of reward and punishment is developed especially in Greek sources.

c. Judgment Scenes. While all the apocalypses refer to a judgment, and a few describe the place of judgment (*1 Enoch* 27) or the preparations for it (*1 Enoch* 53), JUDGMENT SCENES are relatively rare in the otherworldly journeys. The scene in *1 Enoch* 62 conforms to the judgment scenes of the "historical" apocalypses. In *Testament of Abraham,* however, an elaborate scene focuses on the judgment of individuals rather than the condemnation of peoples. Here Abel sits on the throne of judgment. There are two recording angels (Recension A), a motif reminiscent of Zechariah 3, where the angel of the Lord and Satan oppose each other at the trial of the high priest Joshua. *Testament of Abraham* also has the characteristically Egyptian motif of the weighing of the souls. Antecedents for this type of judgment scene have been sought in Orphism, as reflected in Plato's *Gorgias* and *Republic* Book 10 (the *Myth of Er*) and in Egyptian tradition as represented by the Book of the Dead of Pamonthes and the Tale of Satni-Khamois. (See G. W. Nickelsburg, "Eschatology in the Testament of Abraham: A Study of the Judgment Scene in the Two Recensions," in *Studies on the Testament of Abraham* [ed. G. W. Nickelsburg; Missoula: Scholars Press, 1976] 23-64.)

d. Throne Visions. The apocalyptic visions of the divine throne clearly draw on a prophetic tradition, illustrated in the story of Micaiah ben Imlah in 1 Kings 22 and in the visions of Isaiah 6 and Ezekiel 1. The judgment scene in Daniel 7 includes a throne vision, although no ascent is implied. In the otherworldly journeys THRONE VISIONS are found in *1 Enoch* 14 *(Book of the Watchers)*; 60, 71 *(Similitudes)*; *Testament of Levi* 5; *2 Enoch* 20–21; and *Apocalypse of Abraham* 18 (also *Life of Adam and Eve* 25). The essential motifs of this form are simply that God is seated on a throne and surrounded by angels. The simplest formulation is in 2 Kings 22. God is portrayed as an aged figure in Daniel and *1 Enoch.* The motif of fire plays an important role in the visions of Ezekiel and Daniel (cf. the smoke in Isaiah) and also in *1 Enoch* 14 and 71 and *Apocalypse of Abraham* 18. The angels sing God's praise in Isaiah. Their refrain is repeated in the long recension of *2 Enoch* 21. There is a lengthy angelic hymn in *Apocalypse of Abraham* 17. The *Similitudes* add a distinctive development in that another figure besides God is enthroned in glory ("that Son of Man" or the "Chosen One"; see esp. *1 Enoch* 61–62). Enthronement of the "Son of Man" figure may also be implied in Daniel 7, but it is not explicitly asserted or described. An intriguing throne vision is attributed to Moses in the drama of the Hellenistic Jew Ezekiel on the Exodus (preserved in Eusebius *Praeparatio Evangelica* 9.28; 29.4-16). There the figure seated on the throne rises and yields it to Moses. This composition may be as early as 200 B.C.

Descriptions of throne visions continue in the early Christian apocalypses (most notably in Revelation 4) and become an important element in the tradition of Merkavah mysticism. (See further Gruenwald; Rowland, "Visions.")

e. Lists of Vices. Individual apocalypses may naturally include several literary forms which are well known elsewhere but are not especially characteristic of the apocalyptic genre. An example which is found in more than one apocalypse is the lists of sins for which people are damned in *2 Enoch* 10:4-6 and *3 Bar.* 8:5; 13:4. Lists of Vices, and corresponding lists of virtues, are very common in the Hellenistic world. They are characteristic of Greek popular philosophy but are taken over by Paul and Philo. They are also found in *Testaments of the Twelve Patriarchs*. These lists were not originally or necessarily related to revelatory contexts but were simply vehicles of moral teaching. (See A. Vögtle, *Die Tugend- und Lasterkataloge im Neuen Testament* [NTAbh 16/4.5; Münster: Aschendorff, 1936]; H. Conzelmann, *1 Corinthians* [tr. J. W. Leitch; Hermeneia; Philadelphia: Fortress, 1975] 100-101.)

Bibliography

H. W. Attridge, "Greek and Latin Apocalypses," in *Semeia 14: Apocalypse: The Morphology of a Genre* (ed. J. J. Collins; Missoula: Scholars Press, 1979) 159-86; H. D. Betz, "The Problem of Apocalyptic Genre in Greek and Hellenistic Literature: The Case of the Oracle of Trophonius," in *Apocalypticism in the Mediterranean World and the Near East* (ed. D. Hellholm; Tübingen: Mohr, 1983) 577-97; H. Bietenhard, *Die himmlische Welt im Urchristentum und Spätjudentum* (WUNT 2; Tübingen: Mohr, 1951); W. Bousset, "Die Himmelsreise der Seele," ARW 4 (1901) 136-69, 229-73; J. J. Collins, "The Genre Apocalypse in Hellenistic Judaism," in *Apocalypticism in the Mediterranean World and the Near East* (ed. D. Hellholm; Tübingen: Mohr, 1983) 531-48; C. Colpe, "Die 'Himmelsreise der Seele' ausserhalb und innerhalb der Gnosis," in *Le Origini dello Gnosticismo* (ed. U. Bianchi; Leiden: Brill, 1967) 429-47; A. Dieterich, *Nekyia: Beiträge zur Erklärung der neuentdeckten Petrusapokalypse* (3rd ed.; Darmstadt: Wissenschaftliche Buchgesellschaft, 1969); F. T. Fallon, *The Enthronement of Sabaoth: Jewish Elements in Gnostic Creation Myths* (Leiden: Brill, 1978) 38-57; I. Gruenwald, *Apocalyptic and Merkavah Mysticism* (Leiden: Brill, 1980); M. Hengel, *Judaism and Hellenism* (tr. J. Bowden; Philadelphia: Fortress, 1974) 1.175-218; M. Himmelfarb, *Tours of Hell: An Apocalyptic Form in Jewish and Christian Literature* (Philadelphia: University of Pennsylvania, 1983); W. Morfill and R. H. Charles, *The Book of the Secrets of Enoch* (Oxford: Clarendon, 1896); C. Rowland, "Visions of God in Apocalyptic Literature," JSJ 10 (1979) 138-54; J. Schwartz, "Le voyage au ciel dans la littérature apocalyptique," in *L'Apocalyptique* (Paris: Geuthner, 1977) 89-126; A. F. Segal, "Heavenly Ascent in Hellenistic Judaism, Early Christianity and their Environments," ANRW II.23.2 (1980) 1333-94; M. E. Stone, "Lists of Revealed Things in the Apocalyptic Literature," in *Magnalia Dei: The Mighty Acts of God* (*Fest.* G. E. Wright; ed. F. M. Cross, W. E. Lemke, and P. D. Miller, Jr.; Garden City: Doubleday, 1976) 414-52; D. W. Suter, "*Māšāl* in the Similitudes of Enoch," JBL 100 (1981) 193-212; J. VanderKam, *Enoch and the Growth of an Apocalyptic Tradition* (CBQMS 16; Washington: Catholic Biblical Association of America, 1984).

II. Setting and Intention

The question of the social setting of the apocalyptic genre is inevitably bound up with that of the dates and historical contexts of the actual texts. Any discussion of the setting of apocalyptic literature must take account of the fact that the historical situations of the texts are concealed by the device of pseudonymity. So the *Enoch* literature is given a fictional setting before the flood, Daniel in the Exile, etc. The aftermath of the destruction of Jerusalem is especially popular (Daniel, 4 Ezra, *2* and *3 Baruch*). In the "historical" apocalypses it is often possible to discover the actual time of composition with some precision from the latest historical events mentioned in the *ex eventu* prophecy. The otherworldly journeys are much more difficult to pin down, and we often have to rely on more general evidence, such as their affinity with other literature.

The apocalyptic genre as defined here first emerged in Judaism in the Hellenistic age. Some have argued that the matrix of the genre, or at least of the phenomenon of apocalypticism, should be sought in the late sixth century B.C. Paul Hanson's influential book, *The Dawn of Apocalyptic,* is concerned mainly with the eschatology of the postexilic prophets. Third Isaiah who prophesied a new heaven and a new earth (Isa 65:17) is regarded as "proto-apocalyptic," and the tensions within the Jewish community after the Exile are thought to constitute the original generative matrix of apocalyptic thought—the "dawn of apocalyptic" is located in the circles of visionaries who were excluded from power by the hierocracy. Even in the matter of eschatology, however, Third Isaiah is still closer to preexilic prophecy than to Daniel or *Enoch,* although the continuity of the tradition should not be denied. The apocalyptic interest in the judgment of the dead is not yet in evidence. The so-called Apocalypse of Isaiah (Isaiah 24–27) is closer to the apocalypses in its highly mythological language, but even here the material is presented in the form of oracles and cannot be regarded as an apocalypse. On the other hand, Hartmut Gese has argued that the visions of Zechariah form the oldest apocalypse. From a form-critical point of view it is apparent that the vision form in Zechariah is indeed a transitional link between preexilic prophetic visions and apocalyptic dream visions, although at most "its form as an apocalypse is inchoate" (Knibb, 176). It is not so readily apparent that the content of Zechariah shares the characteristic worldview of the apocalypses.

Even in the case of Zechariah the affinity with the apocalypses lies in the use of one literary form, the dream vision. Antecedents for other characteristic forms, such as the otherworldly journey, must be sought outside the biblical tradition. We have seen that the various component forms of the apocalypses are quite diverse in their origin and prehistory. Babylonian and Persian influences mingle with the biblical (and some Canaanite) traditions in the early apocalypses of *Enoch* and Daniel. Greek influences become more apparent later, in works such as *Testament of Abraham*. The matrix of this amalgam of forms and traditions was the Hellenistic age, when the Jews were freely in contact with other traditions, both east and west. Like the Jews, the Persians and Babylonians had been deprived of national independence and were exposed to new cultural influences, and so there was also some similarity of circumstances throughout the Hellenistic Near East (Smith).

The more specific settings of the apocalyptic literature have often been conceived along the lines formulated by P. Vielhauer (p. 598): "The home of Apocalyptic is in those eschatologically excited circles which were forced more and more by the theocracy into a kind of conventicle existence. In their eschatological expectation, dualistic ideas and esoteric thought these have a certain connection with the Qumran community; in their organization, materials and forms they have a certain connection with "Wisdom" circles. The origin and, in particular, the history of these circles are not yet clear." Vielhauer's formulation was influenced in part by the work of O. Plöger, whose view of the sociological matrix of apocalypticism was similar to that of Hanson. Other popular theories have tried to link the development of the genre with the Hasidim of the Maccabean period or the early Essenes (Hengel), or have seen it primarily as a response to persecution. All these views are now in need of substantial qualification.

The first point which must be emphasized in regard to the setting of the genre is that the apocalyptic literature is not all the product of a single movement; in fact, not all apocalypses necessarily have a *Sitz im Leben* in a movement or community at all. The strongest case for an apocalyptic movement can be based on the early *Enoch* literature—"The chosen righteous from the eternal plant of righteousness" (93:10) designates a special group. The insistence on the solar calendar in the *Astronomical Book* supports the assumption of a separatist community (although the status of the solar calendar in the 3rd century B.C. is still disputed). Again, the "righteous" in the *Similitudes* and the *maśkîlîm* in Daniel can reasonably be taken as group designations. However, the position of Daniel on the Maccabean revolt seems contradictory to that of the *Animal Apocalypse*. *4 Ezra* and *2 Baruch* reflect a quite different theological tradition from either Daniel or *1 Enoch*. They also lack any distinctive group designation and do not appear to express the ideology of any special movement. A work like *Testament of Abraham* is even less bound to a particular group and may be viewed as a reflection on the nature of righteousness.

In view of this situation, no more than a few apocalypses could be assigned to the Hasidim or early Essenism. The Enochic *Apocalypse of Weeks* and *Animal Apocalypse,* and also *Jubilees,* are compatible with what we know of the Hasidim, but in fact that is very little. There is no independent evidence that the Hasidim of the Maccabean period shared the speculative interests of the *Enoch* books. Early Essenism remains a very problematic category. While copies of Daniel and the early *Enoch* books were preserved at Qumran, these apocalypses do not attest either the distinctive beliefs (e.g., dualism) or community structure of the scrolls, and there is no clear case of an apocalypse composed at Qumran (but cf. 4Q Visions of Amram). Neither Daniel's *maśkîlîm* nor the "righteous" of *Enoch* can be simply equated with the early Essenes.

The view that apocalyptic literature had its setting in conventicles is related to the supposed esotericism of these writings. The people who wrote the apocalypses were certainly learned, as can be seen from the wealth of material to which they allude. They were sages rather than prophets in that they sought a comprehensive understanding of the world, although their "wisdom" was very different from that of Proverbs or Sirach. Here again we must allow that the "wisdom" of the *Enoch* circle was rather different from that of 4 Ezra and 2 Baruch. We must assume that an inner circle was aware of the fiction of pseudonymity, while the wider public was not, but the esotericism of these writings has been greatly exaggerated. It was necessary to assume that writings which were attributed to ancient figures such as Enoch had been kept secret over the centuries, but the apocalyptic writers were now divulging the mysteries. This is evidently the case in Daniel, where the wise teachers are said to instruct the "many." It is also true in the much quoted passage in 4 Ezra 14, where Ezra is told to "keep the seventy books that were written last, in order to give them to the wise among the people." If 4 Ezra itself is representative of this hidden wisdom, it is now being made public. The *Enoch* circle may have constituted a relatively closed community, but its relation to the rest of the Jewish society remains uncertain.

The popular view that apocalypses are reactions to persecution is based primarily on the canonical apocalypses of Daniel and Revelation, and is erroneous even in the latter case. The *Book of the Watchers* was written before the time of Antiochus Epiphanes and shows no evidence of persecution. The apocalypses written after the fall of Jerusalem (4 Ezra, *2* and *3 Baruch*) are, again, not reactions to persecution. It is true, however, that all the apocalypses are related to a crisis, but the crises are of different kinds: persecution in Daniel, apparently culture shock in the *Book of the Watchers,* the injustice of history (4 Ezra), the inevitability of death *(Testament of Abraham).* It should also be borne in mind that the crises are *perceived* crises, and may not have been so perceived by everyone (Nickelsburg).

The intention of the genre is closely related to the setting. Vielhauer proposed that the apocalypses were written for the strengthening of conventicle communities, but in fact many apocalypses address a broader audience. Usually they offer consolation and exhortation in the face of some crisis (Hartman, Hellholm). The content of the exhortation, or the kind of stance advocated, may vary; e.g., an apocalypse may support either militant revolution or quietism. The stance of a particular document varies with the tradition from which it comes (Wilson). The consolation and exhortation are sometimes made explicit in the parenetic sections, but usually they are conveyed indirectly, through the view of the world revealed in the apocalypse. The imminence of the judgment in the "historical" apocalypses and the rewards and punishments of the dead in the otherworldly journeys often frame the message of the apocalypses. More broadly the apocalypses provide a comprehensive view of the cosmos through the order of the heavens or the predetermined course of history. This revelation puts the problems of the present in perspective and provides a basis for consolation and exhortation. The intention of an apocalypse then is to provide a view of the world that will be a source of consolation in the face of distress and a support and authorization for whatever course of action is recommended, and to invest this worldview with the status of supernatural revelation. The worldview may or may not serve as the ideology of a movement or group.

Bibliography

In addition to the contributions of Hartman, Hellholm, Hengel, and Vielhauer listed above, note J. J. Collins, "Jewish Apocalyptic against Its Hellenistic Near Eastern Environment," *BASOR* 220 (1975) 27-36; idem, "The Apocalyptic Technique: Setting and Function in the Book of the Watchers," *CBQ* 44 (1982) 91-111; H. Gese, "Anfang und Ende der Apokalyptik, dargestellt am Sacharjabuch," *Theologie und Kirche* 70 (1973) 20-49; P. D. Hanson, *The Dawn of Apocalyptic* (rev. ed.; Philadelphia: Fortress, 1979); M. A. Knibb, "Prophecy and the Emergence of the Jewish Apocalypses," in *Israel's Prophetic Heritage. Essays in Honour of Peter Ackroyd* (ed. R. Coggins, A. Phillips, and M. Knibb; Cambridge: Cambridge University Press, 1982) 155-80; G. W. Nickelsburg, "Social Aspects of Palestinian Jewish Apocalypticism," in *Apocalypticism in the Mediterranean World and the Near East* (ed. D. Hellholm; Tübingen: Mohr, 1983) 639-52; O. Plöger, *Theocracy and Eschatology* (tr. S. Rudman; Richmond: John Knox, 1968); J. Z. Smith, "Wisdom and Apocalyptic," in *Religious Syncretism in Antiquity* (ed. B. Pearson; Missoula: Scholars

Press, 1975) 131-56; R. R. Wilson, "From Prophecy to Apocalyptic: Reflections on the Shape of Israelite Religion," in *Semeia 21: Anthropological Perspectives on Old Testament Prophecy* (ed. R. C. Culley and T. W. Overholt; Chico: Scholars Press, 1982) 79-95.

III. Related Genres

Two other genres of Jewish literature in the Hellenistic period are often grouped with the apocalypses and require a brief comment: oracles and testaments.

Oracles

An ORACLE is inspired speech, cited directly. It is a basic subgenre of prophetic speech. The main Jewish and Christian oracles of the Hellenistic and Roman periods are found in the *Sibylline* collection. The sibyl is, of course, a pseudonym. The content of the oracles has much in common with the apocalypses, especially with the "historical" type. *Sibylline Oracles* 4 is dominated by an *ex eventu* prophecy of history, which is divided into ten generations and four kingdoms. It concludes with an eschatological prophecy including the resurrection of the dead. The difference between *Sibylline Oracles* 4 and an apocalypse lies in the manner of revelation. Eschatological oracles are also attested outside of Judaism in this period, e.g., the Egyptian Potter's Oracle and the Persian Oracle of Hystaspes. These oracles were frequently vehicles of political propaganda but could also be used to convey moral and religious exhortation.

Testaments

A TESTAMENT is a discourse delivered in anticipation of imminent death. The speaker is often a father addressing his sons or a leader addressing his people. The testament begins by describing the situation in which the discourse is delivered and ends with an account of the speaker's death. The actual discourse is delivered in the first person.

The content of a testament may vary, but some of the Jewish testaments resemble the "historical" apocalypses. The *Testaments of the Twelve Patriarchs* are of course pseudonymous. They display a consistent pattern of (a) historical retrospective, (b) ethical exhortation, and (c) prediction of the future. The future predictions often have an eschatological finale. The *Testament of Moses* has an extensive *ex eventu* prophecy and eschatological conclusion. Some testaments are also embedded in apocalypses. *2 Enoch* 58–67 contains a speech of Enoch to his sons followed by his translation to heaven. *2 Baruch* 43–47 gives the last instruction of Baruch to his people, but the passage does not conclude with his death. Likewise, the address of Enoch to his sons in the so-called *Epistle of Enoch* is not followed by the death or translation of Enoch. Nonetheless, there is evidently a close relation between the testament form and the patriarch's report of his revelations, especially when told to his sons. The testament form lends itself especially to moral exhortation, and the eschatological predictions often serve to frame the message.

Bibliography

D. E. Aune, *Prophecy in Early Christianity and the Ancient Mediterranean World* (Grand Rapids: Eerdmans, 1983); J. J. Collins, "Sibylline Oracles," "Testaments," in *Jewish-*

Writings of the Second Temple Period (ed. M. Stone; Philadelphia: Fortress, 1984); A. B. Kolenkow, "The Genre Testament and Forecasts of the Future in the Hellenistic-Jewish Milieu," *JSJ* 6 (1975) 57-71; G. W. Nickelsburg, *Jewish Literature Between the Bible and the Mishnah* (Philadelphia: Fortress, 1981); E. von Nordheim, *Die Lehre der Alten. I: Das Testament als Literaturgattung im Judentum der hellenistisch-römischen Zeit* (Leiden: Brill, 1980).

DANIEL

CHAPTER 1
THE BOOK AS A WHOLE

BIBLIOGRAPHY

W. Baumgartner, *Das Buch Daniel* (Giessen: Töpelmann, 1926); M. A. Beek, *Das Da-nielbuch: Sein historischer Hintergrund und seine literarische Entwicklung* (Leiden: J. Ginsberg, 1935); A. Bentzen, *Daniel* (2nd ed.; HAT 1/19; Tübingen: Mohr, 1952); B. S. Childs, *Introduction to the Old Testament as Scripture* (Philadelphia: Fortress, 1979) 608-23; J. J. Collins, *The Apocalyptic Vision of the Book of Daniel* (HSM 16; Missoula: Scholars Press, 1977); M. Delcor, *Le Livre de Daniel* (SB; Paris: Gabalda, 1971); C. Gaide, *Le Livre de Daniel* (Paris: Mame, 1969); J. G. Gammie, "The Classification, Stages of Growth, and Changing Intentions of the Book of Daniel," *JBL* 95 (1976) 191-204; H. L. Ginsberg, *Studies in Daniel* (New York: Jewish Theological Seminary, 1948); D. W. Good-ing, "The Literary Structure of the Book of Daniel and its Implications," *Tyndale Bulletin* 32 (1981) 43-79; L. F. Hartman and A. A. DiLella, *The Book of Daniel* (AB; Garden City, N.Y.: Doubleday, 1978); E. W. Heaton, *The Book of Daniel* (Torch Bible Commen-tary; London: SCM, 1956); G. Hölscher, "Die Entstehung des Buches Daniel," *ThStKr* 92 (1919) 113-38; K. Koch (with T. Niewisch and J. Tubach), *Das Buch Daniel* (Darmstadt: Wissenschaftliche Buchgesellschaft, 1980); A. Lacocque, *The Book of Daniel* (tr. D. Pellauer; Atlanta: John Knox, 1979); J. C. H. Lebram, "Perspektiven der gegenwär-tigen Danielforschung," *JSJ* 5 (1974) 1-33; A. Lenglet, "La structure littéraire de Daniel 2-7," *Bib* 53 (1972) 169-90; J. A. Montgomery, *A Critical and Exegetical Commentary on the Book of Daniel* (ICC; New York: Scribner's, 1927); M. Noth, "Zur Komposition des Buches Daniel," *ThStKr* 98/99 (1926) 143-63; O. Plöger, *Das Buch Daniel* (KAT 18; Gütersloh: G. Mohn, 1965); N. W. Porteous, *Daniel* (2nd ed.; OTL; Philadelphia: West-minster, 1979); H. H. Rowley, *Darius the Mede and the Four World Empires* (2nd ed.; Cardiff: University of Wales, 1959); idem, "The Unity of the Book of Daniel," in *The Servant of the Lord and Other Essays on the Old Testament* (London: Lutterworth, 1952) 237-68; O. H. Steck, "Weltgeschehen und Gottesvolk im Buche Daniel," in *Kirche* (*Fest.* G. Bornkamm; ed. D. Lührmann and G. Strecker; Tübingen: Mohr, 1980) 53-78; J. Steinmann, *Daniel* (Paris: Cerf, 1950); R. R. Wilson, "From Prophecy to Apocalyptic: Reflections on the Shape of Israelite Religion," in *Semeia 21: Anthropological Perspectives on Old Testament Prophecy* (ed. R. C. Culley and T. W. Overholt; Chico: Scholars Press, 1982) 79-95.

THE BOOK OF DANIEL presents a number of anomalies which are familiar to every student of the Bible.

First, Daniel was regarded as a prophet already in antiquity (Matt 24:15; Josephus *Ant.* 10.11.7 § 266) and is classified with the Major Prophets in the

27

LXX. Yet in the Hebrew Bible it is found in the Writings, in the fourth place from the end (before Ezra, Nehemiah, and Chronicles).

Second, the extent of the canonical text is a matter of dispute, since the Greek translations include four passages which are not found in the Hebrew: the Prayer of Azariah and the Song of the Three Young Men in ch. 3 and the stories of Susanna and of Bel and the Dragon. The "additions" are included in the canon of the Roman Catholic Church, but regarded as apocryphal by Protestant Christianity. There is little doubt that these passages were added after the Hebrew-Aramaic book had been completed, but nevertheless they show that there can be no simple appeal to the "canonical form" of the text, at least in an ecumenical context. They also illustrate the diachronic factor in the composition of Daniel and the impossibility of isolating the canonical text from the study of tradition.

Third, even within the text of the Hebrew Bible, Daniel is anomalous by its bilingualism. Chapters 1:1–2:4a and 8–12 are in Hebrew, while chs. 2:4b–7:28 are in Aramaic.

Fourth, the problem of the two languages is compounded by the formal variety of the book. Chapters 1–6 are basically stories, which refer to Daniel in the third person. (Chapter 3 does not refer to him at all.) Chapters 7–12 are ostensibly revelations about the future, presented by Daniel in the first person. The division of the book at 7:1 is corroborated by the dating sequence of the chapters. Chapters 1–6 are set in the reigns of Nebuchadnezzar (chs. 1–4), Belshazzar (ch. 5), and Darius the Mede (ch. 6). Chapters 7 and 8, however, revert to the reign of Belshazzar, followed in sequence by Darius (ch. 9) and Cyrus of Persia (ch. 10). The most perplexing anomaly lies in the fact that the division on the basis of form and date does not coincide with the division on the basis of language. (The argument of Gooding, that the book should be divided at 6:1, fits neither the formal nor the linguistic data.)

Finally, there is the discrepancy between the surface impression gained by a precritical reading and defended by conservative scholarship and the understanding proposed by modern critical scholarship. On the surface, chs. 1–6 tell a series of stories about Jewish exiles in Babylon in the sixth century, one of whom was the recipient of the revelations which are presented in chs. 7–12. The impression that Daniel was the author of the book is derived from the first-person accounts in chs. 7–12 and the direct address of the angel in 12:4, "you, Daniel, shut up the words, and seal the book." By contrast, modern scholarship has held that Daniel is a legendary figure, that the stories in chs. 1–6 are no older than the Hellenistic period, and that the revelations in chs. 7–12 were written in the Maccabean period when the Syrian king Antiochus Epiphanes was persecuting the Jews.

The authenticity of Daniel is a sensitive theological question over which heated battles have been waged, beginning with the famous critique of Porphyry and the response of Jerome. Much of the debate has centered on matters of historical reference, such as the historicity of Darius the Mede, or on the a priori possibility of predictive prophecy. Neither of these issues is directly relevant to a form-critical commentary, and in any case the essential points have been made repeatedly (e.g., in Rowley's classic *Darius the Mede and the Four World Empires*). Underlying the debate, however, is the fundamental question of the genre (or genres) of Daniel. Nebuchadnezzar and Cyrus of Persia were unquestionably historical figures, but the stories in which they are mentioned are not for that reason factual. One can grant the a priori possibility of predictive prophecy without conceding that we find it in Daniel. In each case we must decide what *kind* of story we are dealing with: historical account or edificatory legend, bona fide prediction or *vaticinium ex eventu* (prophecy after the fact). These are literary and form-critical questions. They carry theological implications but they cannot be decided on theological grounds.

Moreover, a form-critical examination bears directly on all the introductory problems noted above.

The place of Daniel in the Hebrew Bible is most probably due to the fact that the prophetic canon was closed before the book appeared. The more significant issue, however, is whether Daniel properly belongs with the Writings. The dominant view of critical scholarship is that Daniel is not a prophetic book but an apocalypse, and is the only full-fledged exemplar of its genre in the Hebrew Bible.

Irrespective of the date at which the Greek "additions" were attached to Daniel, the question of their coherence with the book remains. Here it may be said that Bel and the Dragon is more germane to the book than Susanna, although it is at best out of sequence. Also the Song of the Three Young Men is more appropriate in its context than the Prayer of Azariah is. It is apparent that a purely synchronic study of Daniel must regard at least some of the "additions" as extraneous material. Here the need for some supplementary diachronic study becomes clear.

The diachronic development of the book is also at issue in the problem of the two languages. The most plausible explanation is that an original collection of Aramaic stories was expanded by the addition of the Hebrew revelations in chs. 8–12. This much has been generally accepted, despite H. H. Rowley's famous defense of the unity of the whole book. (The view that the book was a unity was dominant prior to Hölscher's work in 1919. See the review in Koch, *Daniel*, 59-66.) Some scholars hold that the entire book was composed in Aramaic at different times, and that chs. 8–12 were translated for reasons of nationalistic fervor (Ginsberg, Hartman and DiLella). This theory does not explain why only these chapters were translated. The earliest textual evidence, from the Qumran scrolls, already shows the transitions between the two languages. The place of 1:1–2:4a and of ch. 7 in the development of the book is still disputed.

Hölscher proposed three basic stages (with several later interpolations):

(1) Chapters 1–6, all in Aramaic, third century.
(2) An enlarged Aramaic book, chs. 1–7, third century.
(3) Expansion to chs. 1–12 in the Maccabean era.

A variant on this schema has

(1) The original collection is chs. 2–6.
(2) The second stage included ch. 7 and possibly 1:1–2:4a in Aramaic.
(3) The third included the Hebrew chs. 8–12 and 1:1–2:4a in Hebrew, either as a new composition or as a translation from the Aramaic (so Steck, 54-55).

29

Yet another variant is proposed by Gammie (p. 195):

(1) 2:4b–7:18 (less 7:7b-8, 11a, 12).
(2) 1:1–2:4a; ch. 10; 12:1-4.
(3) 7:19-28; chs. 8, 9, 11; 12:5-13; 7:7b-8, 11a, 12.

Crucial to all these proposals is the reconstruction of a pre-Maccabean stratum in Daniel 7. This issue involves the internal structure of that chapter and will be discussed in the commentary below. For the present it must suffice to say that the arguments for an earlier stratum are not compelling. The referential aspects of the book suggest that chs. 7–12 belong together in the Maccabean period since all are dominated by the persecution of Antiochus Epiphanes. By contrast, chs. 1–6 contain no certain allusions to that time. While some episodes in chs. 1–6 *could* be read as allegories for the persecution, the overall portrayal of the Gentile kings is scarcely compatible with the persecutor of chs. 7–12.

Daniel 7 is presented as the earliest of the visions and was possibly written before the desecration of the temple in December 167 B.C., since it does not clearly reflect that event. It is possible that this chapter was added to the Aramaic tales before the composition of the Hebrew chapters, but if so the interval would have to be very short, perhaps only a few months. It is easier to suppose that all the visions were added at the same time by the editor who gave the book its final shape (in the Hebrew-Aramaic form). We must assume that both the editor and the intended audience were bilingual. The editor may well have been the author of the Hebrew visions.

The use of two languages in the composition of Daniel can be explained from the diachronic development. The retention of the two languages in the final edition of the book, however, must be explained in terms of the structure as a whole. The retention of Daniel 7 in Aramaic serves as an interlocking device between the two halves of the book. Chapter 7 belongs with the visions by genre, subject matter, and fictional dating (since it begins a new sequence of Babylon-Media-Persia). It is linked to the tales by language and by the obvious parallelism with the four-kingdom prophecy of ch. 2. As Lenglet has noted, chs. 2–7 form a chiastic structure in which 2 and 7 are related by the four-kingdom schema, 3 and 6 are tales of deliverance, and 4 and 5 offer critiques of the kings. This formation does not prove that the Aramaic chapters originally formed an independent book, but it does testify to careful editorial arrangement. It has been suggested that chs. 3–6 once circulated independently, since the LXX of these chapters differs in character from the rest of Daniel (Montgomery, 37; Koch, 19). The parallelism between ch. 7 and ch. 2 not only expands the chiasm but provides a correspondence between the beginnings of the two halves of the book.

The opening section, 1:1–2:4a, was either composed in Hebrew as an introductory chapter for the entire book or translated from Aramaic. Since it would seem to be presupposed in chs. 2–6, and in no way reflects the Antiochean persecution, it was more probably part of the original Aramaic collection. Since it is preserved in Hebrew it is set off from the other tales and forms an inclusio with the Hebrew visions at the end.

Structure

I. The Tales	1:1–6:29 (*RSV* 6:28)
A. Introductory narrative (Babylonian era, Hebrew)	1:1-21
B. The story of Nebuchadnezzar's dream (Babylonian era, Aramaic)	2:1-49
C. The story of the fiery furnace (Babylonian era, Aramaic)	3:1-30
D. The story of Nebuchadnezzar's madness (Babylonian era, Aramaic)	3:31–4:34 (*RSV* 4:1-37)
E. The story of Belshazzar's feast (Babylonian era, Aramaic)	5:1–6:1 (*RSV* 5:31)
F. The story of the lions' den (Median era, mention of Persian; Aramaic)	6:2-29 (*RSV* 6:1-28)
II. The Visions	7:1–12:13
A. The vision of the beasts from the sea and the "Son of Man" (Babylonian era, Aramaic)	7:1-28
B. The vision of the ram and the he-goat (Babylonian era, Hebrew)	8:1-27
C. The interpretation of Jeremiah's prophecy (Median era, Hebrew)	9:1-27
D. The angel's revelation (Persian era, mention of Greek era; Hebrew)	10:1–12:13

On the basis of the diachronic analysis given above, it is assumed that Part I originally circulated as an independent collection of tales (with ch. 1 in Aramaic).

The position of ch. 1 is ambiguous. It is included with the tales here since it involves a court tale and was probably originally an introduction to chs. 2–6. Yet it is set apart from the other tales by its language and serves now as an introduction to the whole book. The wise teachers who play a crucial role in ch. 11 are called *maśkîlîm*, a term applied to Daniel and his companions in ch. 1.

Again, the conclusion in 12:5-13 serves both as a conclusion to the last vision and to the book as a whole. Formally, however, it is part of the final vision rather than a separate unit.

The two halves of the book are each marked by a sequence of Babylonian, Median, and Persian rulers. The sequence is notable for its inclusion of Media and reflects the four-kingdom schema of chs. 2 and 7. The fourth kingdom— Greece—is mentioned in ch. 10. This structuring device, with the alternation of Hebrew and Aramaic, serves to bind the book together in an editorial unity.

The tales in Part I may have circulated as individual stories before they were collected or may have been developed from older tales (see the discussion of the relationship of Daniel 4 to the Prayer of Nabonidus below). We have noted the chiastic arrangement of chs. 3–6 and the suggestion that these chapters may once have circulated as a separate unit. The three young men, however, have an integral role only in ch. 3. Their association with Daniel is presumably due to the collector of the tales, and is established in chs. 1 and 2.

The opening chapter provides the framework for the following stories and is presumably the work of the editor who gathered or adapted them. It establishes the identity of Daniel and his friends and the parameters of Daniel's career. The statement that Daniel continued until the first year of Cyrus (1:21) is echoed in a looser reference in 6:29. Chapter 1 also prepares for ch. 5 by explaining how the vessels came to be in Babylon. The dating of ch. 2 to the second year of Nebuchadnezzar is meant to set it near the beginning of Daniel's career, and accounts for his rise to prominence. It also provides for the elevation of his friends. Chapter 3 is exceptional in making no mention of Daniel. The only thread of continuity to the next chapter is the name of the king, Nebuchadnezzar. (The traditional story underlying ch. 4 was about Nabonidus.) Chapter 5 is linked to ch. 4 since Belshazzar is thought to be the son of Nebuchadnezzar, and the stories provide contrasting examples of the pride and humiliation of kings. Chapter 5 ends with the capture of Babylon by Darius the Mede, thus setting the stage for the reorganization of the empire which is the point of departure for ch. 6. The concluding reference to Daniel in 6:29 reaches to the end of Daniel's career. The stories, then, are clearly arranged in chronological order, and assume a sequence of Babylonian, Median, and Persian empires. There is no attempt in the tales, however, to associate Daniel with the fourth kingdom foretold in ch. 2.

The visions, in chs. 7–12, are more obviously bound to each other, by their consistent focus on the reign of Antiochus Epiphanes. Chapters 7 and 8 are very closely related. Both are set in the reign of Belshazzar, therefore in the Babylonian period but not in the earlier reign of Nebuchadnezzar, to which chs. 1–4 were ascribed. The chronological framework of the visions overlaps with the tales, but begins later and extends further. Chapter 8, like ch. 7, is a symbolic dream vision. The image of the little horn is common to both. The statement at the end of ch. 8, that Daniel did not understand the vision, opens the way for further revelations. Chapter 9 is dated in sequence to the reign of Darius the Mede. The main analogy with ch. 8 lies in the apparition and discourse of a revealing angel. The substance and imagery of the angel's communication is rather different from the other visions because of the explicit reliance on an older biblical prophecy. There is no concluding formula to smooth the transition to the next section. It may be that ch. 9 is meant to provide a break and change of perspective before chs. 10–12, which are closely related to ch. 8. Chapters 10–12 do not have a symbolic vision, but the apparition of the angel is similar to ch. 8, and the content of the revelation in each case speaks of an assault on heaven by the king. Chapters 10–12 are more detailed both in their historical allusions and in their eschatology, and they build up to a climactic revelation of resurrection in ch. 12. This is the only unit dated to the reign of Cyrus of Persia, to his third year, although ch. 1 had Daniel continue only to Cyrus's first year (1:21). The supplementary vision in 12:5-13 is in the nature of an epilogue. The statement that "the words are shut up and sealed" (12:9) marks the conclusion not only of that unit but of the entire book.

Despite the chronological progression in both the tales and the visions, the relation between the units is not simply sequential. Chapters 3 and 6 provide variations on a theme of miraculous deliverance. Chapters 4 and 5 illustrate the theme of pride and humiliation. All the visions are concerned with essentially the same events—the persecution of the Jews by Antiochus Epiphanes. The final revelation is the most detailed, but it in no way supersedes those that go before it. Rather, the different visions look at the same events from different angles.

Taken together they provide a more fully rounded picture than any one of them alone.

Genre

Taken as a whole, Daniel is an APOCALYPSE, by the definition given in the discussion of that genre above. More specifically it belongs to the subgenre "HISTORICAL" APOCALYPSE, which does not involve an otherworldly journey, but is characterized by *ex eventu* prophecy of history and by eschatology that is cosmic in scope and has a political focus.

The revelation is given in the form of allegorical visions in chs. 7 and 8 and in angelic discourses in chs. 9 and 10–12. The visions are also interpreted by an angel. The content of the revelation has a review of history, in the guise of prophecy and an eschatological crisis, in each unit. Daniel 12 explicitly speaks of the resurrection of the dead. The importance of the heavenly world is shown in the vision of the divine throne in ch. 7 and the roles of angels and holy ones in chs. 7, 8, and most explicitly in chs. 10–12.

That Daniel combines a number of revelations, each of which could be regarded as an apocalypse in itself, is not unusual. This is also true of 4 Ezra, 2 Baruch, and the *Similitudes of Enoch*. Apocalypse is a macrogenre which provides the frame holding various smaller forms together. The overarching unity of Daniel is shown by the narrative framework, which establishes Daniel's identity in chs. 1–6 and in ch. 12 tells him to seal up the book, as if it were all a single revelation. More unusual is the extent of the narrative framework, which is not an ad hoc composition but incorporates a collection of traditional stories which were originally composed for a different setting. The use of legendary narratives as introductory material is not without parallel—cf., e.g., *Apocalypse of Abraham, Testament of Abraham, 2 Baruch,* or even the myth of the fallen angels in *1 Enoch.* It has even been proposed that such narratives are an intrinsic part of the genre (Rowland, 49-52). What is unusual in Daniel is the use of a *collection* of stories and the ideological tensions between them and the subsequent revelations. Yet in the final form of Daniel these stories definitely serve as an introduction to the revelations, and the dominant form of the whole is an apocalypse.

While the subgenres of chs. 1–6 are quite distinct from those of 7–12, there are some significant continuities in both form and content. Daniel is presented in the tales as a recipient of revelations and as a skilled interpreter of dreams and mysteries. Chapters 7–12 are preoccupied with such revelations, although Daniel is no longer the interpreter. There are affinities in content between the four-kingdom passages in chs. 2 and 7, and the miraculous deliverance in chs. 3 and 6 is obviously relevant to the situation described in ch. 11. Yet it would be far too simple to view chs. 7–12 as merely "filling in the details of the early visions of Daniel through the study of scripture and thus confirming Daniel's prophecies in the light of the events of contemporary history" (Childs, 616). The apocalyptic forms in chs. 7–12 represent a quite new development over and beyond the dream interpretation of ch. 2, and the motifs which carry over from the tales do not determine either the form or the message of the revelations. Only in the case of Daniel 9 can we speak of a midrash, and then the base text is not taken from Daniel 1–6 but from Jeremiah. The attempt to present the revelations simply as an outgrowth of the tales is an apologetic strategy intended to mitigate

33

the supposed scandal of pseudonymity. In fact, however, pseudonymity is a constant feature of the Jewish apocalypses and should cause no surprise here.

The classification of Daniel as an apocalypse is fraught with theological implications. The significance of the genre label is that it points to a context for the interpretation of the individual text. In the case of Daniel, the generic context is provided primarily by pseudepigraphic works, the various apocalypses in *1 Enoch,* *4 Ezra, 2 Baruch*. There is no clear case of another apocalypse in the Hebrew Bible. This is not, of course, to deny the massive literary influence of the biblical tradition: we need mention only the analogies with the Joseph story, or the influence of Ezekiel and Zechariah on the vision form. Yet the total *Gestalt* of Daniel finds its best parallels in the Pseudepigrapha, and it is in that context that we must understand its literary conventions and function. In short, Daniel cannot be adequately interpreted within the context of the canon alone. In the past, commentators have tried to avoid this conclusion by dismissing the noncanonical apocalypses as Daniel's "second-rate imitators." We now know that several parts of *1 Enoch* are likely to be older than the revelations of Daniel, and there is surely no reason to regard a book like 4 Ezra as "second-rate." When due account is taken of the genre, then such matters as pseudonymity and *ex eventu* prophecy are no longer theological problems, but conventions which indicate the nature and function of the book.

Setting

Any discussion of an apocalypse must distinguish between the ostensible setting which is given in the text and the actual settings in which it was composed and used.

Ostensibly, Daniel is set in the Exile in the sixth century, at the successive courts of Babylonian, Median, and Persian kings. The fictitious character of this setting has been demonstrated at length by Rowley and others. The main point at issue in this debate is not so much the date of the tales (which are traditional stories in any case) but the authenticity of the predictions in chs. 7–12. Here it must be said that the evidence of the genre creates a great balance of probability in favor of the critical viewpoint. If the historical "predictions" of *Enoch* are recognized as *ex eventu,* the burden of proof must fall on those who wish to argue that Daniel is different from the other examples of the genre.

The Setting of the Tales

The ostensible setting of Daniel is not without significance, however. In Daniel 1–6 it creates a paradigmatic setting, to exemplify how Jews can preserve their religious integrity in the service of Gentile kings. The most probable time of composition of these stories is the third or early second century B.C. The four-kingdom sequence, which is explicit in Daniel 2 and is implied by the introduction of Darius the Mede before Cyrus of Persia, points to a date in the Hellenistic period (under the Greek kingdom). The allusion to intermarriage in 2:43 most probably refers to one of the dynastic marriages between the Ptolemies and the Seleucids. The Greek names of instruments in ch. 3 also suggest the Hellenistic period. Since there is no clear allusion to Antiochus Epiphanes in the tales we must assume that they were composed before the events of his reign. It is likely, however, that these tales had a long prehistory. The origin of these traditions is most naturally to be sought in the eastern Diaspora. Whether they attained their present form there or in Judea is less certain. There is no doubt that the revelations were composed in Judea and so we must assume that the tales were brought back from the Diaspora at some point.

Any attempt to identify the social setting of the tales must of necessity be hypothetical. We may distinguish three ways of approaching the problem.

First, some scholars "accept the narratives' own description of the group involved" (Wilson, 88). According to the text, Daniel and his companions were upper-class Jews who had been educated to serve in the royal court and were entrusted with administrative responsibilities in the Babylonian and Persian empires. We cannot, of course, assume that all aspects of the story reflect the circle of the authors. There is evidently an element of fantasy in the degree to which these Jews are honored and promoted. Yet we might assume that these stories reflect the aspirations and concerns of upper-class Jews in the eastern Diaspora. The authors may have been bureaucrats or counselors, educated in "the letters and language of the Chaldeans." At the same time they were pious Yahwists, concerned not to compromise their religion while serving their king. They regarded the Gentile courtiers and wise men as their colleagues. There is no hint of rebellion in these stories. Problems may arise through professional rivalry (in chs. 3 and 6) but the king is generally benevolent. Even the blasphemous Belshazzar in ch. 5 promotes Daniel in the end. These stories reflect the interests of Jews who were successful in the Gentile world, and who stood to gain by maintaining the status quo.

The second line of approach is congruent with the first, and concerns the intellectual tradition reflected in the tales. Daniel and his companions are wise men, but their wisdom is different from that of Proverbs or Sirach. Rather, it is the mantic wisdom of the Babylonian wise men, who were skilled in the interpretation of dreams and mysteries. Some strands of the Hebrew Bible had looked askance at dreams as a mode of revelation (Deut 13:2-4 [*RSV* 1-3]; Jer 23:28; 27:9; 29:8; Sir 31[34]:1-8; 40:5-7). The approval of dreams here, at least as revelation for Gentiles, has a precedent in the Joseph story, but may nonetheless indicate Babylonian influence. While the authors' knowledge of the history of the Babylonian era was defective, they were familiar with a wide range of lore, as can be seen from the symbolism of the dream in Daniel 2.

The third line of approach is not so directly related to the ostensible setting of the tales. O. H. Steck has noted the affinity between the tales and the ideology of the Jerusalem theocratic establishment in the postexilic era (Steck, 57-58). The theocracy existed within the framework of the world-empires, Persian and Greek, and so was interested in affirming that these empires were subject to the control of the God of the Jews. The "wisdom circles" in Jerusalem might also be learned in international lore and aspire to surpass the Chaldean wise men. Steck draws further support for this thesis from the hymnic passages, which resemble the hymnody of the Jerusalem temple. The interest in the temple vessels in chs. 1 and 5 and the fact that Daniel opens his windows toward Jerusalem in ch. 6 might also be construed as favoring this hypothesis.

Steck's hypothesis has merit in so far as it cautions against the assumption that the ostensible setting of the tales is necessarily the setting of the authors. Yet the evidence for the proposed "wisdom circles" in Jerusalem is scanty indeed. We know of one major representative of Jerusalem wisdom in the pre-Maccabean era—Ben Sira. The interests and attitudes of that sage are poles apart from those of Daniel, and the evaluation of dreams in the two works is directly contradictory. While the attitudes of the tales are conceivable in the case of the Jerusalem theocracy, nothing in these stories demands a Jerusalem setting. The hymnic tradition of the Psalter must have been known to Jews outside Judea in the post-exilic period. Interest in the temple itself is lacking: the temple vessels figure prominently only in the story of Belshazzar's feast. It is not apparent why Jerusalem circles should develop a cycle of tales set in Babylon, especially when the heroes were not prominent in the biblical tradition. The hypothesis of a setting in the eastern Diaspora remains more plausible.

On any reckoning, the authors of the tales were learned people, presumably from the upper classes. They may have used oral materials to fashion their tales, but the end product was definitely literary in character. They saw themselves as participants in the life of the Gentile empires of the day and were content to recognize those empires as established, for the present, by their God.

The Setting of the Visions

By contrast with the elusiveness of the tales, we have exceptionally clear indications of the historical provenance of the revelations. Porphyry noted in antiquity that the predictions in Daniel 11 are correct down to (but not including) the death of Antiochus Epiphanes, but thereafter incorrect or unfulfilled. Analogy with other historical apocalypses supports the conclusion that these "prophecies" were actually written during the time of persecution but before the king's death, or at least before his death was reported in Jerusalem. The date of composition thus may be set between the profanation of the temple in 167 and the end of 164 B.C. We need not suppose that all the revelations were composed simultaneously. The Aramaic ch. 7 may be slightly older than the Hebrew chapters. It may even have been written before the desecration of the temple, but after the outbreak of the persecution. Attempts to pinpoint the date of individual chapters to specific months have not carried conviction. It is sufficient to know that the visions have their setting in the time of persecution and that the tales were now re-read in the light of this new setting.

The setting of Daniel can be specified further in that the author evidently identifies with the *maśkîlîm* or wise teachers who play a crucial role in Daniel 11. As we have noted above, Daniel is said to be a *maśkîl* in ch. 1. The *maśkîlîm* are the heroes of the persecution and they will shine like the stars in the resurrection (12:3). It is more difficult to say just who these *maśkîlîm* were. In the scholarly literature they are often identified with the Hasidim who are known from 1 and 2 Maccabees. However, the Hasidim were mighty warriors who supported Judas Maccabee vigorously until Alcimus was appointed high priest. There is no militant ideology in Daniel. From the title *maśkîlîm* we may infer that they were teachers.

It is reasonable to suppose that there was continuity between the authors of Daniel 1–6 and the circle which produced the visions. This assumption is supported by the fact that Daniel and his companions are *maśkîlîm* in all wisdom in 1:4. The heroes of ch. 11 are thus associated with the heroes of the Exile. While the tales are congruent with the visions in significant respects (the deliverance from death, the idea of mysterious revelation) it is not apparent that the *maśkîlîm* of the Maccabean era would have picked up the older Diaspora tales if they had not been conscious of continuity with the tradents of these tales. We may suppose then that the authors of the visions were learned people, and indeed the visions show a good knowledge of Hellenistic history and familiarity with ancient mythological imagery. By virtue of their education they presumably belonged to the urban upper class, although they were not necessarily wealthy. They may have made their living by teaching, as Ben Sira also did. We do not know at what point this group returned from the Diaspora to Jerusalem.

The main alternative to viewing the *maśkîlîm* as wise men or scribes (in a tradition different from Ben Sira) is the proposal of Lebram that the book of Daniel was written by priestly circles in Jerusalem. Presumably these circles would have been sympathetic to Onias III rather than to the Hellenistic reform. Lebram's main argument is that the temple plays a central role in Daniel and that the disruption of the cult is the author's primary concern. He also argues that the periodization of history and the cosmic scope of the book are priestly characteristics. This thesis would fit well with Steck's theory that the tales originated in the Jerusalem theocracy, although the two theories are independent of each other. It is not apparent, however, that Daniel's visions are dominated by the temple to the degree that Lebram claims. The great vision in ch. 7 does not even refer to it explicitly. The profanation of the temple by Antiochus imprinted itself on the minds of all Jews of the age, as we can see from the books of Maccabees. When the temple was threatened again in the time of Caligula, the Alexandrian Jewish philosopher Philo wrote a powerful protest in his *Legatio ad Gaium*. A similar reaction is recorded in the Egyptian Jewish work 3 Maccabees. Neither Philo nor the author of 3 Maccabees belonged to the Jerusalem priesthood. There is no reason to suppose that only priests were interested in the periodization of history or cosmic chronology. If the book was written by priests we would expect a clearer attempt to establish the priestly character of the *maśkîlîm* in ch. 11. Some cultic language is used in connection with their death, but the characterization of the *maśkîlîm* emphasizes their wisdom and their role as teachers.

The visions show a greater affinity with the prophetic tradition than do the tales, especially in the development of the vision form and the interest in eschatology. The shift in interest is presumably due to the new situation and does not require a change in the make up of the group. Steck has also argued for influence from Levitical circles with a strongly Deuteronomic theology. We will consider this suggestion in the commentary on ch. 9.

The precise place of the *maśkîlîm* in the spectrum of Jewish society at the time of the persecution is less than clear. There is no evidence that they supported the Maccabees. They can be aligned with the Hasidim only if that group is understood more broadly than 2 Macc 14:6, which associates them with Judas, would suggest, although they may have had much in common with those pious scribes. They must also be distinguished from the apocalyptic group that produced the *Enoch* literature. There is no evidence that they were pro-Egyptian or would have followed Onias IV when he withdrew to Egypt. It would appear that they were quietists, concerned to preserve purity and to commune with the angelic world. Yet they took an active role in resisting Antiochus, not by fighting but by spreading the revelations contained in these visions. The material was circulated in written rather than in oral form, but may have been supplemented by oral teaching.

The book of Daniel was so widely accepted that it eventually became part of the Hebrew Bible. This should perhaps warn us against identifying the authors too closely with any sectarian group such as the founders of the Qumran sect, although the book was copied at Qumran and has numerous points of contact with the scrolls (cf. the use of such terms as *pesher* and *raz,* the use of *maśkîl* as title for an office, and the apparent influence of Dan 11:21-35 on 1QM 1). The Qumran community drew on other strands of tradition too. In any case the book of Daniel was not written for insiders but was meant to help the masses understand. Its subsequent influence shows that it transcended the particular concerns of the group that produced it.

Intention

The intention of Daniel in its historical setting is surely to exhort and console the faithful Jews in the face of persecution. The tales of chs. 1–6 could also serve that intention, especially the stories of the fiery furnace and lions' den. In their original setting, however, the tales provided a "life-style for the Diaspora" that showed how fidelity to the Jewish law and service of the king could be combined.

It is useful here to distinguish between the message of the book and the technique by which it is communicated. The content of the exhortation is complete fidelity to the Jewish law, even at the risk of death. This message is constant throughout the book and is exemplified by Daniel and his companions as well as by the *maśkîlîm.* The context of fidelity, however, is different in the two parts of the book. In the tales, the context is the service of the Gentile kings, which is not so much commended as assumed. In chs. 7–12 the context is confrontation with pagan power and there is no question of reconciling the kingdom of God with that of Antiochus. In this context Daniel's message acquires a more specific nuance of pacificism. The *maśkîlîm* are to lay down their lives, but there is no hint of militant resistance. The techniques by which the message is conveyed vary with the context. The tales arouse a sense of wonder and the miraculous, and suggest that fidelity even at the risk of death may prove paradoxically to be the key to advancement. The revelations hold no such easy optimism. Instead they require belief in a supernatural world populated by angels and revealed through dreams and visions. The resolution of human problems must be sought in this supernatural world, and ultimately it involves not miraculous preservation from death but resurrection and exaltation in an afterlife.

Throughout the book the kingdom of God provides the frame for human history. In the tales this is acknowledged primarily in the doxologies. God "removes kings and sets up kings" (2:21), although this is understood consistently only by the wise, like Daniel, who are privy to revelations. In the end God will set up a kingdom which will never be destroyed (2:44), but for the present he has given dominion to the world-kingdoms (cf. Jer 27:5-7). In the visions, the human kingdoms, at least in their final manifestation, are in revolt against God, but divine sovereignty is affirmed, again through special revelations. The kingdom is given to "the people of the saints of the Most High." The formulation here suggests that there is another dimension to human history. The kingdom is given in a heavenly judgment, and the "saints" or angels play a role in it (most obviously in the case of Michael in chs. 10–12). There is evident continuity between the two halves of the book, but the new situation calls for increased emphasis on the supernatural.

The fictitious setting of the book in the Exile plays a part in its literary function. It serves to conceal the actual historical situation beneath the paradigmatic crisis of the past. This device helps put the present crisis in perspective. In the revelations it also provides the occasion for *ex eventu* prophecy, and so for the suggestion that all is foretold and thus predetermined. The fictitious setting also opens the book up to repeated applications, long after the crisis under Antiochus Epiphanes had passed. Ultimately the book addresses not only one particular crisis but a recurring type. So, e.g., the prophecy of the four kingdoms could be reinterpreted so that the fourth was not Greece but Rome. The setting and function of the apocalypse then are not exhausted by a single historical referent.

In this regard, the differences between the two parts of the book are significant. The *origin* of these differences can only be explained by the diachronic development of the book: the relations between Jews and Greeks were better when the tales were written than they were when the revelations were written. As the book now stands, however, it addresses two *types* of situation, both of which recur throughout history. These are variant possibilities in life, rather than successive historical situations. The suppression of historical particularity in this case opens the way to universal applicability.

CHAPTER 2
THE INDIVIDUAL UNITS: THE TALES

BIBLIOGRAPHY

A. Aarne and S. Thompson, *The Types of the Folktale* (Helsinki: Suomalainen tiedeakatemia, 1964); W. Baumgartner, "Ein Vierteljahrhundert Danielforschung," *TRu* 11 (1939) 59-83, 125-44, 201-28; G. W. Coats, *Genesis, with an Introduction to Narrative Literature* (FOTL I; Grand Rapids: Eerdmans, 1983); J. J. Collins, "The Court-Tales in Daniel and the Development of Apocalyptic," *JBL* 94 (1975) 218-34; F. C. Conybeare, J. R. Harris, and A. S. Lewis, *The Story of Aḥiḳar* (2nd ed.; Cambridge: Cambridge University Press, 1913); J. G. Gammie, "The Classification, Stages of Growth, and Changing Intentions of the Book of Daniel," *JBL* 95 (1976) 191-204; idem, "On the Intention and Sources of Daniel I-VI," *VT* 31 (1981) 282-92; E. Gerstenberger, "Psalms," in *Old Testament Form Criticism* (ed. J. H. Hayes; TUMSR 2; San Antonio: Trinity University Press, 1974) 179-223; H. Gunkel, *The Legends of Genesis* (tr. W. H. Carruth; New York: Schocken, 1964); R. Hals, "Legend: A Case-Study in OT Form-Critical Terminology," *CBQ* 34 (1972) 166-76; W. L. Humphreys, "A Life-Style for Diaspora: A Study of the Tales of Esther and Daniel," *JBL* 92 (1973) 211-23; A. Jolles, *Einfache Formen* (2nd ed.; Tübingen: Niemeyer, 1958); J. M. Lindenberger, *The Aramaic Proverbs of Ahiqar* (Baltimore: Johns Hopkins University Press, 1983); M. McNamara, "Nabonidus and the Book of Daniel," *Irish Theological Quarterly* 37 (1970) 131-49; A. Meinhold, "Die Gattung der Josephgeschichte und des Estherbuches: Diasporanovelle, I, II," *ZAW* 87 (1975) 306-24; 88 (1976) 79-93; H.-P. Müller, "Mantische Weisheit und Apokalyptik," *Congress Volume, Uppsala* (VTSup 22; Leiden: Brill, 1972) 268-93; idem, "Märchen, Legende und Enderwartung: Zum Verständnis des Buches Daniel," *VT* 26 (1976) 338-50; R. E. Murphy, *Wisdom Literature: Job, Proverbs, Ruth, Canticles, Ecclesiastes, and Esther* (FOTL XIII; Grand Rapids: Eerdmans, 1981); A. L. Oppenheim, *The Interpretation of Dreams in the Ancient Near East* (Philadelphia: American Philosophical Society, 1956); P. von der Osten-Sacken, *Die Apokalyptik in ihrem Verhältnis zu Prophetie und Weisheit* (Munich: Chr. Kaiser, 1969); D. B. Redford, *A Study of the Biblical Story of Joseph* (VTSup 20; Leiden: Brill, 1970); L. A. Rosenthal, "Die Josefsgeschichte mit den Büchern Ester und Daniel verglichen," *ZAW* 15 (1895) 278-84; W. S. Towner, "The Poetic Passages of Daniel 1-6," *CBQ* 31 (1969) 317-26; C. Westermann, *The Praise of God in the Psalms* (tr. K. Crim; Richmond: John Knox, 1965); R. R. Wilson, "From Prophecy to Apocalyptic: Reflections on the Shape of Israelite Religion," in *Semeia 21: Anthropological Perspectives on Old Testament Prophecy* (ed. R. C. Culley and T. W. Overholt; Chico: Scholars Press, 1982) 79-95.

THE GENRES OF DANIEL 1–6

In his review of the literature in 1980 Klaus Koch (*Daniel*) listed no fewer than five categories which have been proposed as overall classifications of Daniel 1–6: MÄRCHEN, LEGEND, COURT TALE, ARETALOGICAL NARRATIVE, and MIDRASH. The profusion of categories is due to two factors: some are simply inappropriate for this material, and others relate to different aspects and levels of the stories.

Koch neglected to mention the broadest and most basic genre of these chapters: the STORY or tale, defined as a narrative which creates interest by arousing tension or suspense and resolving it. This categorization is so obvious that it is usually taken for granted. Conversely, most critical scholars take for granted that the genre is *not* HISTORY. This assumption does not rest on the mistaken allusions to Belshazzar as king of Babylon or to Darius the Mede—inaccuracy is compatible with the genre of history writing! Rather it rests on two observations:

(1) The stories show stereotypical patterns which are paralleled in the folklore of the world. Folklore may of course incorporate historical data, but as Gunkel said so well (*Legends,* 10), its aim is not to inform us of what actually happened but "to please, to elevate, to inspire and to move." Historical accuracy is incidental and not essential to the genre.

(2) The stories frequently introduce marvelous elements, such as the writing on the wall or the transformation of Nebuchadnezzar, which suggest that their purpose is to inspire wonder rather than to record fact. This impression is furthered by the occasional doxologies which express the appreciation of wonder.

The use of marvelous elements to inspire wonder is the point of analogy between the tales in Daniel and the MÄRCHEN. MÄRCHEN is a traditional narrative set in a mysterious world of fantasy, provoking sympathy for the principal figure. The crucial element here is the prominence of the fantasy world. "Fairy tale" is a more appropriate English translation than the broader category "folktale." No one would argue that the narratives of Daniel as they now stand are *Märchen*: their narrative world is predominantly realistic. They do, however, contain *Märchen*-type motifs, such as the writing on the wall. Since several of these stories may have evolved from earlier forms (a process which can be documented in the case of Daniel 4), H.-P. Müller has proposed that they originated as *Märchen*. This hypothesis is hardly necessary. In any case, *Märchen* is not now the appropriate genre label for Daniel 1–6.

The mysterious world of fantasy is also directly relevant to two other categories, the legend and the aretalogical narrative.

The LEGEND may be defined as a narrative primarily concerned with the wonderful and aimed at edification (Murphy, 177; cf. Coats, 8, 318). It has no specific structure as such and is not primarily concerned with narrative interest. It often inculcates awe for holy places or respect for individuals who may be models of virtue. A narrower definition was offered by A. Jolles, who took the corpus of legends about Christian saints as his point of departure. A legend is a narrative which expresses "a virtue embodied in a deed" and focuses on the element of *imitation*. The stories of Daniel 1–6 have been taken as a case in point

(Hals, 173): "They portray the virtue of fidelity embodied in a variety of deeds and they clearly focus on the call to 'go and do likewise.' " The focus on imitation serves to delimit the corpus by exclusion of, e.g., cult legends. The call for imitation is implied clearly enough in Daniel 1, 3, and 6. It is not apparent, however, that when Daniel interprets the king's dream or deciphers the writing on the wall anyone can meaningfully be expected to go and do likewise. By contrast, all the stories fall under the broader rubric of narratives concerned with the wonderful and aimed at edification. That some of the stories focus on heroic individuals (chs. 3 and 6; 1 and 2 to a lesser degree) is also characteristic of those legends that illustrate the lives of the saints.

The ARETALOGICAL NARRATIVE is closely related to legend since it is concerned with the wonderful and miraculous, but legend is the more widely accepted designation.

The relative simplicity of these stories characterizes them as legends rather than as novellas, which typically involve subplots and interweaving motifs. The specific designation "martyr legend," which is often applied to Daniel 3 and 6, is not appropriate since the stories do not involve martyrdom (Beek, 73). It is apparent, however, that the line between legend and aretalogical novella is a very thin one. The aretalogical novella is simply an elaborate legend artfully told.

The COURT TALE is a quite different kind of classification from legend or *Märchen*. It delimits the category "story" by reference to a particular setting: it is the story of adventures at a royal court. Within this category different subtypes of court tale may be distinguished by variations in plot. These plots are found in other folktales besides, without the court setting, and are elaborated in different ways in legends, sagas, or novellas. This classification then cuts across the other form-critical designations, since it is based on setting and plot rather than on the narrative world and intention. It is nonetheless a useful and valid classification, since it indicates the most immediate context of these stories in ancient Near Eastern literature, by pointing up the affinities of Daniel with Joseph, Esther, Aḥiqar, the story of the three pages in 3 Ezra 3, and more broadly with the tales of Near Eastern courts in Herodotus and Ktesias. It should not be regarded as an alternative to "legend" but as a complementary designation which further characterizes the genre of these stories. The genre may be further specified by the subcategories TALE OF COURT CONTEST and TALE OF COURT CONFLICT (Humphreys).

Less useful is the category "Diaspora novella" proposed by Meinhold for Joseph and Esther, although this too has some obvious validity. In fact, Jewish court tales are invariably set in the Diaspora, a fact which is significant for the history of the genre. 3 Maccabees is a late example. This designation loses sight of non-Jewish parallels such as Aḥiqar, but it does have the advantage of focusing attention on the Jewish setting of the tales.

The overall genre of the tales in Daniel 1–6 can then be specified as COURT LEGENDS, or legends in a court setting. The genre of each individual story will be further specified below.

Finally, the category "midrash" should be eliminated from the discussion of these chapters. As noted in the Introduction above, the midrash takes its point of departure in the biblical text and exists for the sake of explaining that text. It is not enough that a work make use of biblical allusions. The characterization of

Daniel 1–6 as midrash has been favored especially by French scholars (e.g., Delcor, Gaide, Lacocque, but see also Hartmann and DiLella). So Gaide regards these tales as midrashim on the Joseph story. The parallels between Joseph and Daniel are well known, but we cannot say that the Danielic tales exist for the sake of explaining that story. The influence of biblical motifs and terminology is a considerable factor in the tales (Gammie, "Intention and Sources"), but it does not determine their genre.

INTRODUCTORY NARRATIVE, 1:1-21

Structure

I. Introduction	1-7
A. Historical introduction	1-2
1. Date	1a
2. Report of events leading to presence of exiles in Babylon	1b-2
a. Siege of Jerusalem	1b
b. Surrender of king and vessels	2a
c. Transportation to Babylon	2b
d. Deposit of vessels in treasury	2c
B. Introduction of protagonists	3-7
1. Royal summons for noble youths	3
2. Characterization of youths	4a-e
3. Provision for youths	4f-5
a. Education	4f
b. Food and drink	5a
c. Duration of education: three years	5b
d. Final objective: to stand before the king	5c
4. Names of youths	6-7
a. Their Jewish names	6
b. New court names	7
II. Rejection of royal food	8-16
A. Statement of problem: Daniel's resolve to avoid royal food	8a
B. Proposal of resolution	8b-14
1. Daniel's petition	8b
2. Response of chief eunuch	9-10
a. Explanatory statement: God made him sympathetic	9
b. His own statement of his fear	10
3. Daniel's proposal of test	11-13
4. Statement of eunuch's consent	14
C. Result of test	15-16
1. Comparison with other youths	15
2. Change of assigned diet	16

Daniel 1 is essentially an introductory chapter which establishes the identity of Daniel, his relation to the three young men, and his standing at court. Since Daniel does not even appear in ch. 3 and the youths are only mentioned incidentally in the other chapters, their association is evidently secondary. The allusion to the removal of the vessels prepares for the story of Belshazzar's feast. The description of Daniel and his companions as *maśkîlîm b*ᵉ*kol ḥokmâ* (1:4) is significant in view of the role of the *maśkîlîm* in ch. 11. In this case the association is probably secondary, since the *maśkîlîm* of ch. 11 are not courtiers like Daniel and his companions. The concluding date to the reign of Cyrus marks the horizon of Daniel's full career. This chapter was probably composed as an introduction to the tales but also serves as an introduction to the whole book.

The introduction to the chapter begins with the (historically inaccurate) date and extends to the list of names in vv. 6-7. Verses 1-2 establish the setting in time and place; vv. 3-7 identify the protagonists.

Verses 8-16 constitute an independent story. Verse 8 is the first sentence in which Daniel is the subject. The theme of this story is the refusal of pious Jews to eat the king's food. This theme is paralleled in other stories from the Diaspora, notably Greek Esther (cf. also Tob 1:11 but contrast 2 Kgs 25:29). The narrative is realistic, and the beneficial effect of the vegetarian diet is not in itself incredible. Yet the implication of the story is that their good health is due, not to the quality of their diet, but to the favor of God. Compare vv. 9 and 17 where God's favor causes the sympathy of the head steward and endows the youths with knowledge. The placing of the food test conveys the implication that the subsequent success of the youths is due to their fidelity. This unit reaches its conclusion when the steward removes the offensive food.

The transition to the concluding statements is marked by the phrase "As for these four youths." The following statements establish their status, first by claiming that God endowed them, then by reporting the approval of the Gentile king. The chapter ends, as it began, with a date.

Genre

The central narrative of the rejection of the royal food in vv. 8-16 determines the genre of the whole. Since the story focuses on the exemplary conduct of Daniel and his friends and the wonderful way in which they succeed, it should be classified as a LEGEND, or more specifically, because of its setting, a COURT LEGEND. The facile way in which they excel strains the realism of the story and evokes a response of wonder. (The king finds them ten times better than the Babylonian courtiers.)

The plot of the story bears some resemblance to Daniel 3 and 6 in that it involves a miraculous rescue. In this case the threat from which the youths are rescued is muted: it lies in their potential embarrassment and consequent coercion to defile themselves by taking unclean food. They are delivered from this threat by the favor of God, who makes the steward indulgent, and, implicitly, causes their health to thrive. Both the danger and the miraculous character of the deliverance are more emphatic in the later chapters, but the pattern of divine protection is already suggested. The motif of court contest is suggested by the comparison with the Babylonian courtiers, but it does not determine the plot.

The story of the youths could be viewed as a fulfillment of Isa 39:7: "And some of your own sons, who are born to you, shall be taken away; and they shall be eunuchs in the palace of the king of Babylon." It is not necessary to assume that Daniel was inspired by this verse, since the story arises naturally enough from the Diaspora experience.

Setting

The narrative setting of Daniel 1 is the Babylonian Diaspora. The opening date betrays the fictional character of this setting: the third year of Jehoiakim (606 B.C.) was prior to the accession of Nebuchadnezzar and long in advance of the capture of Jerusalem. Daniel is apparently relying on 2 Chr 36:5-7, which says that Nebuchadnezzar took Jehoiakim to Babylon, and on 2 Kgs 24:1, which says that Jehoiakim served Nebuchadnezzar for three years and then rebelled. Yet the story has enough "local color" of the Babylonian era to preserve the realistic atmosphere. Daniel and his companions join the ranks of the Babylonian wise men, who are required to master the "letters and language of the Chaldeans" and whose skills include the interpretation of visions and dreams. Elsewhere in Daniel the term Chaldean refers to a class of wise men and diviners (e.g., Dan 2:2-5, 10). This usage is anachronistic. "Chaldeans" came to signify astrologers and diviners in the Hellenistic age (see Diodorus Siculus 2:29-31). If the "letters and language" pertain to this class, rather than to the Babylonians at large, they presumably refer to the omen collections which enjoyed considerable importance in ancient Babylonia.

The historical setting in which Daniel 1 was composed is elusive. It is probable that the individual tales had their separate prehistories and that the three young men were not originally associated with Daniel. Chapter 1, then, was probably composed as an introduction to the collection when the tales were brought together. It is thus a relatively late stage in the evolution of Daniel. An absolute date cannot be established. We might suggest the end of the third century as the approximate period. The insistence on Jewish dietary observance is not attested in Daniel 2–6, but is germane to the Diaspora setting, as we can see from, e.g., Tobit. While the issue of food is not raised in chs. 2–6, these tales maintain a sharp boundary between Jew and Gentile on such matters as idolatry and prayer. The dietary concern does not require a date in the time of Antiochus Epiphanes. Daniel 1 sets a scene where Jews can prosper in the service of a pagan king. Such optimism would be unlikely during the Maccabean crisis.

It is possible that the characterization of Daniel and his companions as noble youths who receive an extensive education is an idealized projection of the author's own circle. It was possible for Jews to rise to prominence at a pagan court, as we know from the case of Nehemiah, who was cupbearer to a Persian king. The issue of dietary observance was likely to present itself to any Jew who moved in court circles. Not all Jews were necessarily as scrupulous as Daniel is here. The story presents an ideal and affirms its possibility by the wonderful means of the legend.

Intention

The tales in Daniel have been said to present "a life-style for the Diaspora" (Humphreys). The exemplary aspect of the stories is well illustrated by ch. 1. It has two aspects. On the one hand, it conforms to the advice of Jer 29:7 to seek the welfare of the city where they dwell. Jews have no compunction about serving a foreign king. On the other hand, the tales insist on full fidelity to the Jewish law. Moreover, these two objectives are firmly bound together. It is precisely Daniel's fidelity to the law that ensures the divine favor and leads to his good health, superior wisdom, and success at court.

Daniel 1 achieves its effect through the use of the legend. The story does not only propose action to be imitated. It presents a view of the world in which such virtuous action is shown to be profitable. It is a world where God rescues and advances his servants in wonderful ways. Within such a world the tension between Jewish law and the expectations of the Gentile court can be resolved. The end and goal of the story is the approval and promotion of the Jewish youths by the king.

THE STORY OF NEBUCHADNEZZAR'S DREAM, 2:1-49

Structure

I. Introduction	1-2
A. Date formula	1a
B. Notice of dream and king's distress	1b
C. Summons of interpreters	2
II. Dialogue between king and Chaldeans	3-12
A. Statement of problem by king	3
B. Request by Chaldeans that king tell dream	4
C. King's response	5-6
1. Threat	5
2. Promise	6a
3. Impossible demand: show me the dream and its interpretation	6b
D. Second request that king tell the dream	7
E. Second response of king	8-9
1. Charge that they are buying time	8-9a
2. Charge of conspiracy to lie	9b
3. Renewal of impossible demand	9c
F. Assertion of impossibility by Chaldeans	10-11
1. Denial that any man can do it	10a
2. Denial that any king has ever asked it	10b
3. Assertion that only the gods can do it	11
G. Conclusion of dialogue	12

C. Promotion of Daniel and his friends   48-49a
   1. King honors Daniel   48
   2. Promotion of friends at Daniel's request   49a
D. Concluding statement ("Daniel remained at
   the king's court")   49b

The introduction indicates the problem and assembles the initial cast of characters. The dialogue between the king and the Chaldeans heightens the tension of the story, building up to the death sentence in 2:12. It also establishes that the problem cannot be resolved without supernatural aid. The report of Daniel's intervention is a transitional section which serves to introduce Daniel in this story and bring him to the presence of the king. The account of his reception of the revelation heightens the supernatural backdrop and again ends with his introduction before the king. Before he proceeds to tell the dream, Daniel again underlines its supernatural source. The climax of the story is Daniel's successful telling and interpretation of the dream. His success, rather than the content of the interpretation, determines the king's extravagant reaction at the end. The promotions of Daniel and his friends set the stage for the following stories.

A few passages have been thought to be secondary (Hartmann and DiLella, 139): (1) Verses 13-23: in v. 16 Daniel goes to the king, yet in v. 25 he is introduced to the king as if he had just been discovered. Verse 47 is closely related to vv. 20-23. The reference to his companions in v. 17 appears secondary, as does the other allusion to them in v. 49. (2) Verses 29-30, like 13-23, explain how the mystery was revealed to Daniel. (3) Verses 41b-43 give three different interpretations of the mixture of iron and clay in the statue's feet: first "a divided kingdom," then "partly strong and partly brittle," and finally dynastic intermarriage.

It is important to clarify what is meant by "secondary" here. The allusion to the three young men in v. 49 was most probably added when the tales were collected. Therefore it is secondary to the original freestanding tale, not to the collection, certainly not to the full apocalyptic book. There is indeed noteworthy similarity between the manner in which Daniel receives his revelation in vv. 14-23 and the apocalyptic revelation in ch. 7 and 8. It is possible then that vv. 13-23 and 29-30 (also 47?) belong to the redaction of the full apocalyptic book of Daniel. (Daniel's reception of revelation is not described in ch. 4.) They add an emphasis to the original story but they change neither its genre nor its function.

In vv. 41-43 the successive interpretations may be understood as explanatory glosses. The first two (divided kingdom, partly weak and partly strong) are complementary. The reference to dynastic marriage may have been added either to the freestanding tale or to the collection.

Genre

Like the other tales in Daniel 1–6, ch. 2 is a COURT LEGEND: a story set in the royal court, concerned with the wonderful, and aimed at edification.

The plot of the tale has been further specified in terms of Aarne and Thompson's folktale type 922, which comes under the heading "Clever Words and Deeds" (Niditch and Doran, 180). The plot structure of this type of folktale is as follows:

(1) A person of lower status is called before a person of higher status to answer difficult questions or to solve a problem requiring insight.

(2) The person of higher status poses the problem, which no one seems capable of solving.

(3) The person of lower status solves the problem.

(4) That person is rewarded for answering.

This plot structure is shared by other COURT TALES, such as Genesis 41 (Joseph) and Aḥiqar, and corresponds to the subgenre TALES OF COURT CONTEST (Humphreys, 217; Collins, *Apocalyptic Vision*, 34), although the type is not necessarily confined to a court setting. In both Joseph and Daniel the problem arises from a dream and the failure of the Gentile wise men is emphasized. (For a somewhat different use of this folktale type see the story of the three pages in 1 Esdras 3–4 and Josephus *Ant.* 11.3.2-6 §§ 33-58. See also, more broadly, De Vries.)

Within the story a number of forms are used in a subsidiary manner. These include:

(1) THE DREAM REPORT. This is anticipated by the opening statement that Nebuchadnezzar had a dream but actually provided by Daniel in vv. 29-35. It is characterized as *ḥlm'* ("dream") and introduced by a formula ("you were looking and behold!"). Daniel 2 is exceptional in that the king refuses to tell his dream. In this respect the folkloric motif of "impossible tasks" is introduced, and the legendary character of the tale is heightened. The apparently secondary comments of Daniel in vv. 27-28 emphasize this aspect of the story.

(2) THE DREAM INTERPRETATION. This is given its own designation, *pesher*. The cognate Hebrew term *pittārôn* is used for dream interpretation in the Joseph story (e.g., Gen. 40:5). The term pesher is also used with reference to the writing on the wall in Daniel 5.

The dream is interpreted symbolically or allegorically, as is common in apocalyptic dream visions. Nebuchadnezzar's dream is not an apocalypse, however, since there is no mediating angel (Daniel is a human interpreter). Nonetheless, the two kinds of dream visions have an obvious affinity, which is underlined in the apparently secondary passage in 2:19: "Then the mystery was revealed to Daniel in a vision of the night."

(3) POLITICAL ORACLE. The actual dream and interpretation constitute an oracle since they are a communication from God to the king through an intermediary (Daniel). Specifically they belong to a class of political oracles, which were common in the Hellenistic age and were concerned with the rise and fall of kingdoms (e.g., the *Sibylline Oracles,* Egyptian Potter's Oracle, Persian Bahman Yasht and Oracle of Hystaspes, Babylonian Dynastic Prophecy). Gentile political oracles too are sometimes communicated in dreams (Oracle of Hystaspes) or visions (Bahman Yasht). These oracles frequently include *ex eventu* prophecy, often with periodization. The specific motif of the four kingdoms is found in *Sibylline Oracles* 4 and the Bahman Yasht (see Flusser). The Babylonian Dynastic Prophecy has also been adduced as a four-kingdom schema (Hasel, 22) since it appears to attest a sequence of Assyria, Babylonia, Persia, and Greece. This sequence is not numbered, however, and there is no indication that the number four is given any definitive status.

The fragmentary 4QpsDaniel from Qumran is closely related to Daniel 2. It presents a summary of world history that Daniel recites "before the ministers of the king." On the reconstruction of the editor (J. T. Milik) it offered a schema of four kingdoms and an eschatological conclusion, but the text is very fragmentary and it is not certain that 4QpsDan[c] belongs to the same work as 4QpsDan[a] and [b]. The affinity with Daniel 2 lies in the court setting and possible use of the four-kingdom schema. The scope of the historical overview is wider, since it begins with the Flood, and if 4QpsDan[c] is part of the same work, it appears to end with a reference to resurrection. This document is later than the final form of Daniel, and is almost certainly influenced by it.

(4) THE DOXOLOGY. The doxology in Dan 2:20-23 has been more specifically designated as "an individual psalm of thanksgiving" (Towner). It is a short hymn of praise. Westermann (p. 102) regards it as a development of the declarative psalm of praise of the individual. It is distinguished from other hymns in Daniel 1–6 by the element of thanksgiving. While it is made up of stereotyped liturgical phrases there is no reason to suppose that it had circulated independently. It is echoed in the brief doxology attributed to the king in 2:47. Both doxologies emphasize that God is a revealer of mysteries and both may have been added at the time of the redaction of the whole Hebrew-Aramaic book.

Setting

The fictional setting is again the Babylonian court. The dating to the second year of Nebuchadnezzar is problematic since it disregards the data of ch. 1, and the second year of Nebuchadnezzar was prior to the Exile in any case. It has been suggested that an earlier form of the chapter was set in the reign of Nabonidus, as is the case in Daniel 4 (McNamara, 145). The discrepancy may simply reflect the disregard for historical precision in these tales.

The dream and its interpretation have also been thought to have had an earlier setting. On one interpretation, the statue originally represented the Babylonian empire and the declining metals represented Nebuchadnezzar and his successors Amel-Marduk, Neriglissar, and Nabonidus (Bickerman, Davies). The mixture of iron and clay would then refer to Nabonidus and Belshazzar, and the final kingdom (a stone that was cut from a mountain, v. 45, and became a great mountain, v. 35) would represent a Jewish eschatological kingdom. On this reconstruction the original setting of the political oracle was in the time of Nabonidus. This view assumes that the interpretation of the dream was altered in the Hellenistic period, since it now clearly refers to a succession of kingdoms. The reference to intermarriage (v. 43) must have been added after the first dynastic marriage between the Ptolemies and the Seleucids (ca. 250 B.C.) or even after the second one (193). This reference may be secondary, but it is questionable whether even the interpretation of the iron and clay as a divided kingdom could refer to Nabonidus and Belshazzar, since the kingdom was not actually divided between them. Moreover, this interpretation disregards the brief (nine-month) reign of Labashi-Marduk, son of Neriglissar, who immediately preceded Nabonidus.

An alternative interpretation sees the political oracle as originally a Babylonian oracle from the Hellenistic age (Collins, "Court Tales," *Apocalyptic Vision*). This interpretation takes its point of departure from the laudatory description of Nebuchadnezzar as the "head of gold." Both the legs of iron and the feet of iron and clay can then be referred to the Greek kingdom, as in the present text of Daniel. The initial kingdom of Alexander was strong as iron but the kingdom was subsequently divided. The final kingdom would most naturally be a return to the "golden age" of Babylonian rule. The enthusiastic reaction of Nebuchadnezzar is more easily intelligible on this interpretation (although a positive reaction is required by the folkloric plot in any case). A parallel for anti-Hellenistic Babylonian prophecy can now be found in the Dynastic Prophecy (Grayson). Babylonian expectation of an eternal kingdom (or dynasty) is attested in the Uruk prophecy. The incorporation of such a Babylonian oracle in Daniel 2 would be an ironic subversion of Babylonian hopes. The national identity of the final kingdom is not explained to Nebuchadnezzar, but he has to rely on a Jew to interpret his dream, and Jewish readers would refer the prophecy to a messianic kingdom.

These proposals are, of course, hypothetical attempts to specify settings for earlier forms of the material in Daniel 2. The Jewish story as we now have it is certainly from the Hellenistic age and was probably (though not certainly!) composed in the Diaspora. If we can assume an analogy with Daniel in the story, the author of the tale was a Jew in the service of a Gentile monarch. He accepted Gentile standards of professional excellence, but in pursuing them sought help from his own religion. Of course, the analogy cannot be pressed. The story is evidently a fiction and represents an ideal rather than social reality. The assumed analogy between Daniel and the author is possible but is not assured. Attempts to specify the setting within the Hellenistic period have not been successful (e.g., Gammie's suggestion that the statue represents the first four Ptolemies does not adequately account for the division of the fourth kingdom).

The literary setting of the chapter is important since it introduces the sequence of kingdoms that is presupposed both in the collection of tales and in the whole book. Though the four kingdoms are not named they can be identified only as Babylon, Media, Persia, and Greece, and this sequence is made explicit by the subsequent references to "Darius the Mede" and Cyrus of Persia. Since Media never ruled over the Jews this sequence can only be explained by supposing that Daniel is adapting the schema of Assyria, Media, Persia, and Greece that is attested in the Roman historian Aemilius Sura and in *Sibylline Oracles* 4 (Swain, Flusser). The introduction of this schema in the first episode of Daniel's career gives perspective to the following stories of Gentile rule.

In the context of Daniel as a whole, ch. 2 anticipates the more intense vision of ch. 7, where the focus shifts definitively to the time of the fourth kingdom.

Intention

It is possible that the political oracle in Daniel 2 originally served as political propaganda. As the chapter now stands, however, the oracle is subordinated to the court legend and serves primarily to display the wisdom which Daniel enjoys by the power of his God. On one level, the message of the story is summarized in the doxologies, especially in the concluding affirmation of Nebuchadnezzar in v. 47: "Truly, your God is God of gods and Lord of kings, and a revealer of mysteries. . . ." By the refusal of the king to tell his dream the contest between Daniel and the Chaldeans is construed as a contest between his God and theirs (cf. v. 11: "none can show it to the king except the gods . . ."). In this respect Daniel 2 recalls the polemic of Second Isaiah against the Babylonian wise men (von der Osten-Sacken, Gammie).

The story not only establishes the superiority of Daniel's God. It also carries a message for Jews, especially in the Diaspora. Daniel does not outshine the Babylonians by his own wisdom but by the power of his God (v. 30). The path to success then is not simply through mastery of the techniques of the Babylonians (although this is not discouraged) but through prayer. It is assumed throughout that Daniel is one among the Babylonian wise men. Daniel 2 then suggests a life-style for those who work in a Gentile setting: only by devotion to their own God can they hope to succeed. The story gives support and encouragement to "the wise" (2:21) but their wisdom is not of the proverbial kind. It is a higher wisdom through revelation.

The political content of the dream and its interpretation appears then to be almost incidental to the message of the chapter, and indeed, Nebuchadnezzar pays scant attention to it. Yet it should not be disregarded. It lends perspective to the situation of the Jews under Gentile rule. We may compare Jer 27:6-7, where God decrees that all nations shall serve Nebuchadnezzar and his son and his grandson, until the time of his own land comes, and then many nations will make him their slave. The oracle is not revolutionary. It encourages patience rather than rebellion. It proposes a view of the world in which Jews can continue in the service of Gentile kings, because they know that Gentile power will not last forever. It appears then that while Daniel 2 uses the plot structure of a folktale, its intention is not to entertain but to convey a religious and in part political message.

In the final redaction of the book the political oracle acquires more weight through the amplification and development of the eschatological prophecy in chs. 7–12. Even then, however, the tale serves primarily to establish Daniel's status as a recipient of heavenly revelation. The heroes of the book are ultimately the wise *maśkîlîm* and these may well be identical with the wise *ḥakkîmîn* referred to in Dan 2:21.

Bibliography

E. Bickerman, *Four Strange Books of the Bible* (New York: Schocken, 1967); P. R. Davies, "Daniel, Chapter Two," *JTS* 27 (1976) 392-401; D. Flusser, "The four empires in the Fourth Sibyl and in the Book of Daniel," *Israel Oriental Studies* 2 (1972) 148-75; A. K. Grayson, *Babylonian Literary-Historical Texts* (Toronto: University of Toronto Press, 1975); G. F. Hasel, "The Four World Empires of Daniel 2 Against Its Near Eastern Environment," *JSOT* 12 (1979) 17-30; S. Niditch and R. Doran, "The Success Story of the Wise Courtier: A Formal Approach," *JBL* 96 (1977) 179-99; J. W. Swain, "The Theory of the Four Monarchies: Opposition History under the Roman Empire," *Classical Philology* 35 (1940) 1-21; J. de Vries, *Die Märchen von klugen Rätsellösern* (Helsinki: Suomalainen tiedeakatemia, 1928).

THE STORY OF THE FIERY FURNACE, 3:1-30

Structure

I. Introductory narrative: report of veneration of statue	1-7
A. Erection of statue	1
1. Description of statue	1a
2. Its location	1b

The introduction again presents the problem and assembles the cast except for the Jewish youths. It also introduces an element of tension, because of the penalty for noncompliance. The compliance of the people in v. 7 might have marked a satisfactory ending of the episode. The accusation against the three Jews sharply heightens the tension. The interrogation by the king highlights the religious issue at stake: who is the god who can save you? Both sections III and IV begin with the notice of the fury of the king. In section V, however, this changes to astonishment. This reaction comes to fuller expression in section VI, in the doxology. The conclusion nicely reverses the fate of the youths. Instead of being destroyed, they are promoted and destruction is threatened for their enemies.

Genre

The character of this court tale as LEGEND is shown by the liberal use of hyperbole (e.g., the height of the statue, the use of *every* kind of music, the destruction of the executioners), the personal involvement of the king and his uncontrolled rage, the astonishment of the king and his confession of the superiority of the God of the Jews. This story also has considerable affinity with martyr legends. The episode in which the youths are brought before the tyrant and questioned directly but respond unflinchingly is especially typical of martyr stories (cf. 2 Maccabees 7).

Here again the plot of the story conforms to a type well known in folklore as "The Disgrace and Rehabilitation of a Minister" (Krappe). Major examples are found in the stories of Joseph, Esther, and Ahiqar. The designation "TALES OF COURT CONFLICT" (Humphreys; Collins, *Apocalyptic Vision*, 49) underlines the motif of rivalry between the courtiers, which is most prominent in Esther, and is clearly present in Daniel 3 and 6 and in Ahiqar. The plot structure is as follows:

(1) The heroes are in a state of prosperity.
(2) They are endangered, often by conspiracy.
(3) They are condemned to death or prison.
(4) They are released, for various reasons.
(5) Their wisdom or merit is recognized and they are exalted to positions of honor.

In Daniel this plot is given the character of a legend by the miraculous element in the preservation of the three men in the fire.

It has been suggested that this legend is simultaneously a MIDRASH on Isa 43:2, "when you walk through fire you shall not be burned" (cf. Ps 66:12; Kuhl, 81; Bentzen, 39, who speaks of *"eine Verkörperung von Sentenzen"*). It has also been noted that in Deut 4:20 the Exodus from Egypt is said to be from "an iron furnace." These biblical allusions testify to the ubiquity of fire as a symbol for mortal danger. (Cf. also the story of Abraham in the furnace in Ps.-Philo *Liber Antiquitatum Biblicarum* 6, a quasi-etymological midrash on his departure from Ur, which is interpreted as fire.) A reader well versed in Scripture could, no doubt, make the association, but there is no indication that Daniel 3 was composed for the sake of elucidating these verses.

The constituent forms or *Gliedgattungen* of Daniel 3 include:

(1) PROCLAMATION in vv. 4-5, which is in the form of a command.

(2) ACCUSATION against the three youths, in vv. 9-12, consisting of a reminder of the decree, and a statement that the Jews do not conform. The peculiarity of this accusation lies in the fact that its force depends on an ad hoc decree, not on established custom or natural law. Hence the opening reminder of the decree.

(3) The INTERROGATION is a typical element in martyr stories, as we have noted.

(4) The DOXOLOGY attributed to Nebuchadnezzar is a brief hymn of praise, which pronounces the blessing and then states the reason (Westermann, 122-23; Gerstenberger, 209).

(5) The royal DECREE in 3:29 is undoubtedly an ad hoc composition, but we have several examples of royal decrees concerning the Jews in the Persian and Hellenistic periods (e.g., those in Ezra 4–7 and the decrees of Antiochus III in Josephus *Ant.* 12.3.3-4 §§ 129-53).

(6) The chapter also contains two LISTS which have a stereotypical character—the list of officials (vv. 2, 3) and the list of musical instruments (vv. 5, 7, 10, 15). The list of officials has been compared with the Babylonian Prism text from the Istanbul Museum (Shea). The difference is that the Babylonian list names the officials, whereas Daniel 3 lacks such specificity.

The Greek translations of Daniel have inserted two lengthy psalms in ch. 3, connected by a brief narrative which further emphasizes the miraculous preservation in the furnace. The first of these psalms is the Prayer of Azariah. This is a COMMUNAL CONFESSION OF SIN and petition for mercy. Similar prayers are found in Psalm 106; Ezra 9:6-15; Neh 1:5-11; 9:5-37; Tob 3:1-6; Dan 9:4-19; Bar 1:15–3:8. The prayer is made up of

(1) confession of God's justice
(2) confession of sin
(3) description of present humiliation
(4) reminder of covenantal promises
(5) renewed description of humiliation
(6) assertion of contrition
(7) prayer for mercy and deliverance.

This prayer, like the others listed above, presupposes a covenantal framework. (See K. Baltzer, *The Covenant Formulary* [tr. D. Green; Philadelphia: Fortress, 1971].) Present distress is a result of breach of covenant. The petition for mercy is based on God's fidelity to his promises and his regard for the fathers and for his own name. The prayer seems singularly inappropriate in its present context since the plight of the three youths is not due to their sin but to their uncompromising loyalty to their God. It may be that the recitation of such a prayer had come to be regarded as a standard act of piety.

The Song of the Three Young Men is less incongruous. It is a HYMN OF PRAISE, which begins with a declarative section, "blessed art thou," and then proceeds to call on the elements to bless the Lord, in the imperative (hence Westermann's designation "the imperative psalms"). The closest parallel is in Psalm 148 (e.g., v. 3: "Praise him, sun and moon"; cf. also Psalms 150, 98, 100). The relevance of this hymn to its context is due to the role of the fire in the preservation of the youths.

Setting

Since Daniel 3 makes no mention of Daniel, it is generally assumed that it originally circulated independently. Various settings have been proposed.

Shea suggests that the story reflects a review of Babylonian officialdom in the wake of an abortive revolt against Nebuchadnezzar in 594 or 593. The obeisance demanded of the officials would then be a loyalty oath. This hypothesis does not explain the role of the statue. It is not impossible that the recollection of such an incident played a part in the formation of the story, but if so Daniel 3 has reinterpreted the test as religious rather than political. The suggestion that Jewish exiles would have ranked among the Babylonian officials at this early date must be considered very doubtful. In short, a *possible* echo of an historical incident in the reign of Nebuchadnezzar cannot be taken as evidence for the historicity of the story in its present form.

A different Babylonian setting for the prehistory of the tale has been proposed by McNamara, who relates it to the religious reforms of Nabonidus, specifically to restoration of the temple of the moon-god Sin at Harran. This involved the reintroduction or restoration of a statue of Sin. The dedication of the temple was a solemn ceremony to which representatives of the whole empire were summoned. We know that Nabonidus's religious policies encountered considerable opposition in Babylon and that the king dealt harshly with his opponents. The fragmentary Verse Account of Nabonidus (*ANET*, 312-14) makes special note of his veneration of the statue of the moon-god. This setting provides a more plausible context in view of the religious character of the confrontation in Daniel 3. It is assumed, of course, that the supposed historical incident is no more than a point of departure for the formation of the Jewish legend.

The fiery furnace was certainly not a standard means of punishment in Babylonia, but several texts suggest that it may have been used. Jer 29:22 refers to "Zedekiah and Ahab, whom the king of Babylon roasted in the fire." Later we read in 2 Macc 13:4-6 that Menelaus, the hellenizing high priest, was executed by being pushed into a tower "fifty cubits high, full of ashes." The story of Croesus, who was miraculously saved from the pyre after he called on Apollo (Herodotus *Hist.* 1.87) has also been adduced as a parallel, as has a Persian story of a sage Sijawusch, who was vindicated through an ordeal by fire (Kuhl, 82-83). None of these provides an exact model for Daniel 3, but the idea of either execution or trial by fire was readily available in any case.

While Daniel 3 may contain reminiscences of the Neo-Babylonian period, there are also indications of later composition. The terminology of the list of officials in vv. 2 and 3 is predominantly Persian in origin and the garments of the youths in v. 21 are Persian. The list of musical instruments contains three loan-words from Greek: *qaytrōs (kitharis), pĕsantērîn (psaltērion)*, and *sûmpōnyâ (symphōnia)*. The last word is first attested as the name of a particular instrument in Polybius in the second century B.C. If "Chaldeans" in this chapter should be understood as the name of a class of wise men, this too is an indication of a Hellenistic date.

A specific setting in the Hellenistic age has been proposed by Gammie, who relates the statue erected by Nebuchadnezzar to that erected by Ptolemy III for his deceased daughter Berenice and recorded in the Canopus Decree, but there is no threat of punishment associated with that statue. There is a very general similarity between the drama of danger and deliverance in Daniel 3 and that of 3 Maccabees, which is set in the reign of Ptolemy IV Philopator, but the specifics of the stories are very different. There is no solid reason to associate Daniel 3 with the Ptolemies in any way. The limited analogy with 3 Maccabees derives from the fact that both stories are set in the Diaspora. All the local color of Daniel 3, however, points to the *eastern* Diaspora.

While we cannot pinpoint the situation in which Daniel 3 was composed, the eastern Diaspora in the Hellenistic period provides the general setting. (The Persian period is also within the bounds of possibility.) The charge against the Jews, that "they do not serve your gods," is one to which the Jews in exile were always vulnerable, especially if they worked in the service of the king. It is echoed directly by Apion, the Alexandrian polemicist of the first century A.D.: "why then, if they are citizens, do they not worship the same gods as the Alexandrians?" (Josephus *Ag.Ap.* 2.6 § 66). A corresponding charge, less obviously religious in focus, is found in Esth 3:8: "their laws are different from those of every other people, and they do not keep the king's laws." We need not suppose that either Daniel 3 or Esther was generated by an actual persecution; it is sufficient that the Jews were aware of the anomaly of their situation and the danger it involved.

The story had obvious relevance to the time of Antiochus Epiphanes. Yet it can scarcely have been composed as an allegory for that situation, since there is very little correspondence in detail. While Nebuchadnezzar is portrayed more negatively than Darius in ch. 6, he is still capable of blessing the God of the Jews. He is far removed from the fourth beast and little horn of Daniel 7–8. When Daniel addresses the persecution of Antiochus in chs. 11–12 he does not posit miraculous preservation from death: the hope of the "wise" is for resurrection after death. The miraculous deliverance of ch. 3 reflects a situation where persecution was possible but not actual, rather than the experience of martyrdom itself. In Christian tradition and art this story was understood as a figure of resurrection, but that is obviously a secondary interpretation (Bentzen, 39).

Intention

The intention of Daniel 3 is to articulate and allay the fears of Jews who worked in the service of Gentiles. The story has a nightmarish quality. The potential for conflict in the Jewish rejection of idolatry is brought to realization. The issue is formulated in strongly religious terms: "who is the god that will deliver you out of my hands?" The conflict is not a test of human wits, as in the folkloric use of this plot structure. It is a test of divine power. It is of course simultaneously a test of the fidelity of the youths, who indicate that they will not worship the image whether their God delivers them or not (v. 18). The resolution of the conflict comes by supernatural power: the king sees a fourth figure "like a son of the gods" walking in the furnace. This figure anticipates the role of the archangel in the apocalyptic visions. Here he is not clearly identified, and so the sense of mystery is enhanced. The conclusion is twofold: the king acknowledges the God of the Jews and threatens anyone who speaks against him with death. The conversion of the king is scarcely less fantastic than the deliverance from the furnace. (Cf. the legend of the deathbed conversion of Antiochus Epiphanes in 2 Maccabees 9.)

Daniel 3, then, is a fantasy in which the potential danger to the Jews is miraculously removed. The end result is not freedom from Gentile rule but royal patronage without reservation. This is the usual aspiration of Jews in the Diaspora—cf. Esther and 3 Maccabees. The desire for vengeance on the enemies is less forceful here than in Esther, but is implicit in the royal decree. Yet, as in Esther, even the vengeance must be sanctioned by the Gentile king.

The story reflects the basic tension in Diaspora life between fidelity to an exclusive God and service to a Gentile king. This tension could be fully resolved only through the conversion of the king, and this could be achieved only in fantasy. The fantasy, however, served a practical purpose. It encouraged Jews to believe that religious fidelity was not only compatible with the royal service, but could ultimately lead to advancement. It also encouraged them to believe that the dangers of their situation were not ultimate. The latter belief, that the power of their God was greater than that of their adversaries, was especially relevant in the Maccabean crisis, when advancement in the royal service was no longer an issue.

Bibliography

A. H. S. Krappe, "Is the Story of Ahikar the Wise of Indian Origin?" *JAOS* 61 (1941) 280-84; C. Kuhl, *Die drei Männer im Feuer* (BZAW 55; Giessen: Töpelmann, 1930); W. H. Shea, "Daniel 3: Extra-Biblical Texts and the Convocation on the Plain of Dura," *AUSS* 20 (1982) 29-52.

THE STORY OF NEBUCHADNEZZAR'S MADNESS, 3:31–4:34
(*RSV* 4:1-37)

Structure

I. Introduction: epistolary prescript	3:31-33 (*RSV* 4:1-3)
A. Epistolary superscription (Nebuchadnezzar to all peoples)	31a
B. Greeting ("Peace be multiplied to you")	31b
C. Reason for writing: to make known the wonders of God	32
D. Doxology	33
II. Report of circumstances (in first person)	4:1-5 (*RSV* 4:4-8)

B. Description of fulfillment	26-30
1. Circumstances: king was boasting	26-27
2. Audition of voice from heaven	28a
3. Decree of heavenly voice	28b-29
a. Address to king	28b
b. Decree of his fate	29a
c. Reason: to learn that the Most High rules	29b
4. Fulfillment of the decree	30
VI. Conclusion of the epistle (first person)	31-34 (*RSV* 34-37)
A. Statement of restoration	31a
B. Doxology	31b-32
1. Benediction	31b
2. Reasons: God's power and dominion	31c-32
C. Further account of restoration	33
D. Final doxology	34
1. Declaration of praise	34a
2. Reason: justice, humiliation of proud	34b

This unit is framed by doxologies at the beginning and end. The report of circumstances at the beginning sets up a contrast between Daniel and the Babylonian wise men. The major transitions are marked by changes of person. The king speaks in the first person, down to v. 15. He is referred to in the third person in the dialogue before the interpretation and again in the account of the fulfillment. The first person resumes in the conclusion, in v. 31.

The report of fulfillment of the prophecy is given in the third person and falls outside the structure of the proclamation. Yet it is a necessary component of the chapter, since without it the conclusion would be unintelligible. The transition to the third person actually takes place at the beginning of the interpretation (v. 16, "the king said . . ."). This inconsistency must be understood in the light of the complex prehistory of the tale, and cannot be simply removed by source criticism. (Cf. the transition in Tob 3:7.)

Genre

The chapter is cast in the form of an EPISTLE from King Nebuchadnezzar to all peoples. The placing of the sender's name before that of the recipient is standard practice in Neo- and Late Babylonian letters, but also in Persian administrative correspondence (the Arsames letters) and is common in Greek epistolography (White, 8). Daniel 4 is exceptional in the corpus of Aramaic letters in that it is a public proclamation—hence an "epistle" rather than a "letter" or means of communication between persons separated from each other, in the terminology of A. Deissmann (*Light from the Ancient Near East* [tr. L. R. M. Strachan; 4th ed.; Grand Rapids: Baker, repr. 1978] 229; see Fitzmyer, 27). The absence of an epistolary conclusion is not unusual in Semitic epistolography. The greeting in v. 2 conforms to epistolary style. The use of the first-person narrator, which is found only here in Daniel 1–6, may be inspired ultimately by the proclamation of Nabonidus in the Harran inscriptions or a similar document. The doxology at the beginning of the epistle is paralleled in some NT passages (2 Cor 1:3-4; Eph 1:3-10; 1 Pet 1:3-5), but note also that the edict in the Harran inscriptions begins with the praise of the god Sin.

The epistolary style is not maintained throughout. The switch to the third person reflects another aspect of the genre of the chapter—it is a LEGEND set in a royal court like the other stories in Daniel. The legendary character of the story is shown by the frequent intrusions of the marvelous: the dream, the voice from heaven, and the miraculous transformations of the king. The edificatory purpose is underlined in the three doxologies.

The main theme of the story is the humiliation and restoration of Nebuchadnezzar. The idea that a pagan king should be brought low because of his pride is popular in the prophetic literature—cf. Isaiah 14 on the king of Babylon, Ezekiel 28 on the king of Tyre (cf. more broadly the theme of reversal in passages such as 1 Samuel 2 or Psalm 107). Bentzen (p. 45) suspected that a common oriental tale of the evil prince lay in the background here. What is noteworthy in Daniel 4, however, is the eventual restoration of the king.

New light has been shed on both the genre and the development of Daniel 4 by the publication of the Prayer of Nabonidus from Qumran (4QPrNab). Only fragments of this document have survived. The "prayer" from which the title is presumably derived is not preserved. The introductory narrative has, however, been pieced together with reasonable success. It is narrated in the first person by Nabonidus, king of Babylon, who says that he was smitten with a bad inflammation for seven years in the city of Tema. Then a Jewish seer, one of the exiles, explained the situation and reproached the king for idolatry. Another passage, which is extremely fragmentary, apparently introduced a dream report in the first person.

The relevance of this discovery to Daniel 4 is obvious. The publication of the Nabonidus Chronicle in 1882 revealed that Nabonidus had been absent from Babylon for several years, and scholars had suspected that the original subject in Daniel 4 was Nabonidus rather than Nebuchadnezzar. 4QPrNab does not provide a direct literary prototype for Daniel 4, but appears to be a variant of the same tradition, which preserves the original name of the king and the association with Tema. The two stories share some basic features: the humiliation and restoration of a Babylonian king, the duration of seven years, the mediating role of a Jewish exile, and probably also the king's dream. Each story fills in the details in a different way.

Both 4QPrNab and Daniel 4 are ultimately based on an account of Nabonidus's withdrawal from Babylon for ten years to the desert oasis of Tema, such as is recorded in the Harran inscriptions. Both stories are considerably removed from the historical report. 4QPrNab posits an affliction of Nabonidus in Tema. The story then becomes a wisdom tale on the problem of suffering in which the affliction of the king is traced to a religious cause, his worship of idols. (See Meyer, 101-4, who compares the framework of Job.) The Jewish character of the story is evident both in the denunciation of idolatry and in the Jewish identity of the seer. The story (at least in the surviving fragments) does not emphasize the miraculous or wonderful. The point of the story is the necessity of worshiping the true God. Nabonidus appears quite well disposed. His sin is due to ignorance rather than to arrogance. By contrast Daniel 4 heightens the supernatural element, especially in the bestial transformation of the king. In this case the affliction is a punishment for pride and a lesson in God's control of the human kingdom. Yet the king seems quite gracious in his dealings with Daniel, and proves to be docile in his distress. The motif of the king's restoration must be seen as a reflection of the original story of Nabonidus, who returned in triumph to Babylon, if only for a short time. This motif, however, is well integrated into the Jewish legend, since it conveys the belief that God will restore even a pagan king if he repents.

Subsidiary Forms

DOXOLOGY. The doxologies in Daniel 4 are HYMNS OF PRAISE. In both cases the pronouncement of blessing ("Blessed be . . .") is replaced by a narrative statement, "and I blessed." The reason for blessing is a generalized statement of God's control over kingdoms and the inhabitants of the earth (cf. Westermann, 123; Gerstenberger, 209).

TALE OF COURT CONTEST. The contest of wisdom between Daniel and the Babylonian wise men, which provided the frame for Daniel 2, is here reduced to a subtheme in vv. 3-6. The plot structure of the typical tale is significantly altered, since Daniel is no longer a person of low degree but already enjoys very high status. His superiority to the Chaldeans is assumed by the king. Therefore the contest is preempted. The main emphasis here is not on Daniel's reception of revelation, but on the fate of the king. (Contrast my earlier treatment in Collins, *Apocalyptic Vision,* 47.)

SYMBOLIC VISION. Unlike Daniel 2, the dream is reported directly by the king. The usual formulas ("I saw, and behold . . .") are employed. The content of the dream is the famous vision of the great tree. Biblical parallels for this image can be found, most notably in Ezekiel 31 and 17:22-24, but the image is very widespread. Babylon is compared to a great tree in the Building Inscription of Nebuchadnezzar (Bentzen, 43). The dream is not, in any case, a midrash on the Ezekiel texts.

The second part of the dream, the decree of the Watcher, strains the imagery in vv. 12-13, where the allegorical interpretation of the tree as a man is presupposed. The Watcher is a mythic-realistic figure; he is not interpreted as a symbol for something else. He functions within the vision as the one who pronounces the sentence, but his role passes over into that of interpreter when he abandons the imagery of the tree and directs, "let his mind be changed," etc. The Watcher then bears some resemblance to the mediating angels of apocalyptic visions. Yet the full allegorical interpretation or PESHER is supplied by the human Daniel. The imagery of the tree does not lend itself naturally to the transformation of the king. It suggests rather the simple downfall of a king or kingdom. It seems probable that the author of Daniel 4 inherited the vision of the tree and the initial sentence of the Watcher, but added the motif of transformation to a bestial state. The specific punishment, a form of lycanthropy, may have been suggested by Jer 27:6, which says that God had given Nebuchadnezzar even the beasts of the field. This point is taken up in the dream in Daniel 4 where the beasts find shade under the great tree. The transformation of Nebuchadnezzar into a beast is then a dramatic inversion of his state. While this conception may have been prompted by the Jeremiah text, it is not a midrash, since it does not exist for the sake of that text, but adds a nuance to the story of the Babylonian king. A possible nonbiblical source for the transformation can be found in a passage relating to Nebuchadnezzar and attributed to Megasthenes (ca. 300 B.C.) by Abydenus and preserved in Eusebius *Praep. Ev.* 9.41.6. There Nebuchadnezzar allegedly prophesied that a "Persian mule" would come to enslave Babylon but that a "son of the Medes" would share responsibility. Nebuchadnezzar wished that the latter figure "might be driven through the desert, where there is no city or track of men, where wild beasts have their pasture and birds roam, and that among rocks and ravines he might wander alone. . . ." The "son of the Medes" is usually identified as Nabonidus, whose mother was Median (Dommershausen, 65). The passage does not suggest that he will be transformed, but the references to the desert and beasts may have suggested the idea. (The allusion to Jeremiah 27 would not necessarily be thereby excluded.)

The inconsistency of the imagery in Daniel 4 suggests that the motif of transformation was added ad hoc to dramatize the reversal of the king's fortunes. It is unfortunate that the dream in 4QPrNab has not been preserved, as this might have given us some control on the traditional form of the dream. As the final composition of Daniel 4 now stands it resembles an apocalypse, both in the use of the symbolic vision and in the political prediction, but is distinguished from that genre by the human interpreter (Daniel) and the lack of any transcendent eschatology.

ADMONITIONS. The interpretation of the dream concludes with admonitions to the king. These are of a highly general nature: "break off your sins by practicing righteousness." Compare Isa 1:16-17, which, like Daniel, links the practice of justice with mercy to the oppressed. Precedent for admonitions to a king in a Babylonian context can be found in the so-called Babylonian *Fürstenspiegel* (W. G. Lambert, *Babylonian Wisdom Literature* [Oxford: Clarendon, 1960] 112-15). The Babylonian literary form is different: it follows the style of omen interpretation with a protasis and apodosis (e.g., "if a king does not heed justice, his people will be thrown into chaos"). The Egyptian Admonitions of Ipuwer (*ANET,* 441-44) also differ in form, since they describe the conditions of the land, rather than admonish directly. It should be noted that the prophecy of the king's downfall is contained in the king's own dream. Daniel only interprets this. He does not independently utter a prophecy (in contrast to the so-called Egyptian prophetic texts, adduced as a parallel by Wilson, 91).

Two other forms in Daniel 4 may be noted briefly. The voice from heaven that addresses Nebuchadnezzar delivers a prophecy or prediction in the form of an ORACLE (i.e., inspired speech reported directly). This is followed by a FULFILLMENT FORMULA: first, a statement that the prophecy was fulfilled (v. 30; cf. v. 25), then a repetition of the prediction.

Setting

We have already seen that Daniel 4 has a lengthy prehistory which goes back to the Neo-Babylonian period. A few points relate to traditions about Nebuchadnezzar. He was famous for his building projects (cf. v. 27). There is also the parallel with the story in Megasthenes of Nebuchadnezzar's prophecy of the fall of Babylon, allegedly delivered on the roof of his palace (cf. v. 26). Despite occasional attempts by conservatives to discover evidence of an illness of Nebuchadnezzar (so G. F. Hasel, "The Book of Daniel: Evidences Relating to Persons and Chronology," *AUSS* 19 [1981] 37-49) the discovery of 4QPrNab shows beyond reasonable doubt that the main theme of the story is derived from a tradition about Nabonidus. The story as we have it in Daniel must be later than the Neo-Babylonian period, in view of the confusion of the two kings and the elaboration of the legendary aspects. Needless to say, the reverence of either Nebuchadnezzar or Nabonidus for the God of the Jews has no basis in history.

At the other extreme, there is no reason to regard Nebuchadnezzar as an allegory for Antiochus Epiphanes. The transformation of the king into a bestial state, which seems to be introduced into the traditional story by the author of Daniel 4, bears some similarity to the portrayal of kings as beasts in Daniel 7. Yet the difference is crucial. In ch. 4 the king is restored to human form and praises God; in ch. 7 the fourth beast is slain and burnt in the fire. While later tradition (2 Maccabees 9) could fantasize the conversion of Antiochus, such an idea is quite incompatible with the way in which he is portrayed in Daniel 7-12.

There is little to indicate the precise date of Daniel 4. A date in the late third or early second century is probable by analogy with the other stories. If Daniel is influenced by the passage in Megasthenes, which is possible but not necessarily the case, this too would support a date after 300 B.C. 4QPrNab preserves an older form of the story in some respects, but Daniel cannot be shown to depend on it, so it does not help specify the date.

The setting, again, is most probably the eastern Diaspora, in some branch of royal service.

Intention

The intention of Daniel 4 is made quite explicit in v. 22: Nebuchadnezzar is told that his humiliation will last "till you know that the Most High rules the kingdom of men, and gives it to whom he will." While this statement is addressed to the king it also states the message for the readers. This message is reinforced by the doxologies on the lips of Nebuchadnezzar that frame the narrative at the beginning and end.

The significance of this message for Jews in the service of a pagan king was that it assured them that their God was in control, despite appearances to the contrary. The same message is found in Jeremiah 27, which states that it is the God of the Jews who gives the sovereignty to Nebuchadnezzar, and also, of course, in Daniel 2. Jews could take comfort from the thought that their God could at any time bring low the pride of their rulers. The king is portrayed as acknowledging the superiority of the God of the Jews, so the Jews themselves need not doubt it. Yet the chapter has no revolutionary intention. At the end of the chapter the king is restored. There is no objection to Gentile rule as such. In the Maccabean period readers may have attended primarily to the humiliation of the king, and this emphasis is encouraged by the treatment of the kings in Daniel 7-12, but the original story is quite universalistic in its account of the king's restoration.

Bibliography

W. Dommershausen, *Nabonid im Buche Daniel* (Mainz: Grünewald, 1964); J. A. Fitzmyer, "Aramaic Epistolography," in *Semeia 22: Studies in Ancient Letter Writing* (ed.

J. L. White; Chico: Scholars Press, 1982) 25-57; C. J. Gadd, "The Harran Inscriptions of Nabonidus," *AnST* 8 (1958) 35-92; R. Meyer, *Das Gebet des Nabonid* (Berlin: Akademie-Verlag, 1962); J. T. Milik, " 'Prière de Nabonide' et autres écrits d'un cycle de Daniel," *RB* 63 (1956) 407-15; W. von Soden, "Eine babylonische Volksüberlieferung in den Danielerzählungen," *ZAW* 53 (1935) 81-89; J. L. White, "The Ancient Epistolography Group in Retrospect," in *Semeia 22: Studies in Ancient Letter Writing* (ed. J. L. White; Chico: Scholars Press, 1982) 1-15.

THE STORY OF BELSHAZZAR'S FEAST, 5:1 – 6:1 (*RSV* 5:31)

Structure

I. Introductory narrative		5:1-6
A. General introduction		1-4
1. Statement that Belshazzar held a feast		1
2. Description of feast		2-4
a. Command that temple vessels be fetched		2
b. Profanation of vessels		3
c. Praise of idols		4
B. Immediate introduction		5-6
1. Appearance of writing		5
2. King's reaction		6
II. Appeal to Chaldeans		7-9
A. Summons of wise men		7a
B. Offer of reward		7b
C. Failure of Chaldeans		8
D. Reaction of king and courtiers		9
III. Speech of queen		10-12
A. Introductory statement		10a
B. Greeting		10b
C. Recollection of Daniel's excellence		11-12a
D. Recommendation: let Daniel be called		12b
IV. Speech of king		13-16
A. Introduction: Daniel was brought in		13a
B. Identification of Daniel and his reputation		13b-14
C. Mention of failure of wise men		15
D. Promise of reward		16
V. Speech of Daniel		17-28
A. Rejection of rewards		17
B. Recollection of story of Nebuchadnezzar		18-21
C. Rebuke of Belshazzar		22-23
1. Lack of humility		22
2. Profanation of vessels		23a
3. Idolatry		23b
D. Interpretation of writing		24-28
1. Affirmation of its divine origin		24
2. Decipherment of the words, introduced by "this is the writing"		25

The introduction gives the story a religious backdrop. The profanation of the vessels sets the scene for what follows. The sudden appearance of the writing on the wall and the king's dramatic reaction build the tension of the story. The failure of the Babylonian wise men is, again, a foil for Daniel's success. The episode closes, as it began, with the alarm of the king. The bulk of the chapter is organized in the form of speeches, by the queen, the king, and Daniel. Daniel's speech refers back directly to ch. 4, and also makes an explicit connection with the profanation of the vessels at the beginning of the chapter. His speech concludes with the actual reading and interpretation, introduced by the formulas "this is the writing" and "this is the interpretation." The reference to the Medes and Persians points forward to the following chapter.

The elevation of Daniel honors the king's promise of a reward, but takes on an ironic quality in the context of imminent disaster. The conclusion "that very night" comes with abrupt finality. The introduction of Darius makes a transitional link to the following story.

Genre

The story of Belshazzar's feast is a straightforward narrative. That it is LEGEND is shown by the marvelous writing on the wall, underlined by the panic-stricken reaction of the king and the moral lesson drawn by Daniel. Like Daniel 2 it resembles Aarne and Thompson's folktale type 922, and, more specifically, conforms to the subgenre TALE OF COURT CONTEST:

(1) The king is confronted with mysterious signs.
(2) The wise men fail to understand.
(3) Daniel succeeds where they fail.
(4) Daniel is exalted to high rank.

As in Daniel 2 and in contrast to Daniel 4, this plot structure provides the frame for Daniel 5. The main variation on this plot here is the insertion of Daniel's indictment of the king. Accordingly Daniel seems to be not only interpreting the writing but also pronouncing sentence. In view of this modification of the traditional story, the elevation of Daniel at the end seems singularly implausible (Daniel had already rejected such honors) and must be attributed to the staying power of the traditional motif (Doran and Niditch). The variation in the plot also explains the story's double ending. The elevation of Daniel is required by the traditional plot structure. The death of Belshazzar and fall of the kingdom are the fulfillment of the sentence pronounced by Daniel.

The story of Belshazzar's feast is composed as a companion piece to that of Nebuchadnezzar's madness. The two are juxtaposed as variations on a theme.

The integral connection between the two is shown by the fact that Daniel recounts the earlier story in 5:18-21. Moreover, ch. 5 shows another point of contact with the Nabonidus tradition as attested in 4QPrNab: in both documents the king is indicted for idolatry, and the list of materials in the Qumran fragment (silver and gold . . . wood, stone . . . clay) corresponds almost exactly with that of Dan 5:23 (bronze and iron may have been included after gold; Daniel does not mention clay).

Bentzen has suggested that the story in Daniel 5 may have been composed as a fulfillment of such prophecies as Isa 21:1-10 or Jer 51:39, 57, both of which speak of feasting in connection with the fall of Babylon. These biblical passages may have suggested the setting of the story, but they do not determine its genre.

Subgenres

The main subordinate forms in Daniel 5 are the INDICTMENT SPEECH and the PESHER.

The indictment speech is used here in a secondary way since it is not in a legal context. Yet Daniel speaks as if he were both bringing an accusation and passing sentence. The pattern of the argument resembles the so-called *rîb* or COVENANT LAWSUIT in the prophetic books (e.g., Mic 6:1-8), although there is no reference to a covenant here. First, Daniel recalls the antecedent history, in this case the story of Nebuchadnezzar. Second, he brings the direct accusation: "you have not humbled your heart . . . ." Finally, the interpretation of the writing conveys the sentence passed on Belshazzar.

The PESHER in this case interprets mysterious writing rather than a dream or a vision, but the technique is the same: the mysterious writing is taken piece by piece and interpreted allegorically. In this case the key to the interpretation is a pun on the mysterious words; cf. the pun on *qyṣ/qṣ* in Amos 8:1-2.

The report of the elevation of Daniel at the end is a FULFILLMENT FORMULA, since it repeats the terms of the promise made by Belshazzar as a statement of what was now done.

Setting

Despite conservative contentions (e.g., Shea) it is impossible to take Daniel 5 as an "eyewitness account" of the fall of Babylon. The problems are well known and concern mainly the figures of Belshazzar and Darius the Mede. Belshazzar (Akk. *Bēl-šar-uṣur*) was son of Nabonidus and not directly descended from Nebuchadnezzar. He commanded Babylon during his father's absence in Tema, but was never technically king. The New Year's Festival in Babylon was simply canceled during the absence of Nabonidus; Belshazzar could not take his place. We do not know what became of him after his father returned to Babylon, or where he was when Babylon was captured.

Herodotus (*Hist.* 1.191) followed by Xenophon (*Cyr.* 7.5) says that Babylon was captured while the inhabitants were distracted by a feast, but in his account this happened after an unsuccessful siege, and after Cyrus had to divert the Euphrates to gain admission. The cuneiform sources, the Nadonidus Chronicle and the Cyrus Cylinder, say that Babylon was captured without resistance after Nabonidus had fled. The king was later captured but his life was spared. Xenophon claims that the Babylonian king was killed when the city was taken, and this has sometimes been understood as a reference to Belshazzar, but Xenophon's reliability is doubtful.

No such figure as Darius the Mede is known to history. Many attempts have been made to identify him with Gobryas (Ugbaru), Cyrus's general who occupied Babylon, but no satisfactory reason has been proposed why he should be called Darius the Mede. The name Darius can be attributed far more plausibly to confusion with Darius I of Persia (522-486). Darius had to put down two revolts by Babylonian pretenders and it is possible that these operations were later confused with the original conquest of Babylon. In Dan 9:1 Darius is said to be the son of Ahasuerus (Xerxes). In fact, Xerxes I was son of Darius. The claim that Babylon was conquered by a Mede may have been suggested by several factors. One is the sequence of the four kingdoms presupposed in Daniel—Babylon, Media, Persia, and Greece. Another is the fact that the Medes were said to destroy Babylon in biblical prophecy: Jer 51:11, 28; Isa 13:17-19; 21:2.

The ostensible historical setting, then, may be based on old traditions, but they are historically inaccurate and confused. We must assume a considerable lapse of time between the fall of Babylon and the actual composition of Daniel 5.

The mysterious writing on the wall is usually assumed to have had a different original meaning. There is a discrepancy between the words which Daniel reads initially, *měnē'*, *měnē'*, *těqēl ûparsîn,* and the words which are subsequently interpreted, *měnē'*, *těqēl,* and *pěrēs.* It is now widely held that the words originally expressed monetary values, which were implicitly applied to the last Babylonian kings, although both the original reading and the precise identifications are disputed. (See the summary in Hartmann and DiLella, 189-90.) It is not certain, however, that the monetary terms were given political significance until the interpretation was added. The last term, *parsîn* or *pěrēs,* suggests the Persians rather than the Medes as the conquerors of Babylon, so the episode of the writing and its interpretation may be older than its present context in Daniel, but it is not possible to reconstruct an earlier form of the story with any confidence.

The present story was probably composed about the same time as Daniel 4 (3rd or early 2nd century). Here again some have seen the king as an allegory for Antiochus Epiphanes (e.g., Rowley). The main point of contact between the two kings is the profanation of the temple vessels. Yet in Daniel 5 the vessels are only the occasion for the idolatrous worship of the gods of gold, silver, etc. The Jewish critique of this worship was well established in the tradition, as we can see from 4QPrNab and even from the polemic against idolatry in Second Isaiah.

Criticism of idolatry was not confined to any one genre or social setting in postexilic Judaism (cf. Isaiah 44; Wisdom 13-15; Bel and the Dragon). The bluntness of Daniel's denunciations is reminiscent of the Hebrew prophets rather than of the Babylonian *Fürstenspiegel,* but is not in itself implausible at a Gentile court. Wilson (p. 91) compares the pattern of Daniel 2, 4, and 5 with the so-called Egyptian prophetic texts, such as the Admonitions of Ipuwer (*ANET,* 441-44), where the sage berates the king for permitting lawlessness and chaos. Since the Egyptian texts were produced by scribes or other members of the Egyptian royal court, Wilson suggests that "Israelite scribes and bureaucrats" might have been familiar with them. The parallels, however, are not close enough to suggest direct influence.

The story in Daniel is, of course, a fiction, intended for a Jewish audience, not an actual prophetic address to a king. It is very unlikely that the author had access to a king in this manner. Daniel could, however, serve as an idealized role model for lesser officials, and urge them, by his fictional example, to reject idolatry and worship the one true God.

There are a few words of possible Greek origin in Daniel 5: *hamônikā'* (7, 16, 29); *kĕrizû* (29). These support the dating to the Hellenistic period, although they do not prove it.

Intention

The message of Daniel 5 is the same as that of the previous chapter, as can be seen from Daniel's indictment, in which the analogy with Nebuchadnezzar plays a central role. The story of Belshazzar is a variation on that of Nebuchadnezzar. It illustrates what happens when a king does not repent. Taken together, the stories show two sides of the Jewish attitude to the Gentile powers. The conversion of the king is desirable, but even if it is not forthcoming, the Jews believe that their God still controls human sovereigns. The historical fall of Babylon could be taken as evidence of this. While these stories encourage the Jews in their faith, they do not advocate rebellion. God will act in his own good time. When the kingdom is taken from Belshazzar it is still given to another Gentile king.

Bibliography

W. H. Shea, "Nabonidus, Belshazzar, and the Book of Daniel: An Update," *AUSS* 20 (1982) 133-49; idem, "Darius the Mede: An Update," *AUSS* 20 (1982) 229-47.

THE STORY OF THE LIONS' DEN, 6:2-29 (*RSV* 6:1-28)

Structure

I. Introduction: report of Daniel's rise to power	2-4
A. Report of reorganization of kingdom	2-3
B. Distinction of Daniel	4
II. Report of conspiracy	5-10
A. Unsuccessful attempts to trap Daniel	5
B. Resolution to seek a religious problem	6
C. Petition to king	7-9
1. Introductory statement: they came to the king	7a
2. Greeting	7b
3. Statement of consensus of officials	8
4. Request for royal signature	9
D. Conclusion: signing of the interdict	10
III. Report of condemnation	11-19
A. Report of Daniel's action	11
B. Accusation	12-14
1. Discovery of Daniel	12
2. Dialogue with king	13
3. Accusation proper	14

The introduction sets the stage by providing the reason for envy toward Daniel. The initiative of the presidents and satraps in v. 4 marks the beginning of a new section, where the trap is set for Daniel. The religious character of the test is emphasized. The next section is introduced by the initiative of Daniel, who acts in defiance of the new law. It culminates with the apparent burial of Daniel in the sealed den and the corresponding distress of the king. The hasty trip of the king to the den begins the story of Daniel's deliverance. Those who had accused him suffer his fate instead. The proclamation of the king provides the immediate conclusion to the story. The notice of the full duration of Daniel's career may have originally marked the conclusion of the tales as a separate collection.

Genre

Several features show the character of the tale to be LEGEND: the unchangeable law, the king's facile compliance with the courtiers, his personal involvement with the attempted execution, the miraculous preservation of Daniel, and the virtual conversion of the pagan king. A major goal of the story is to evoke wonder: "that in all my royal dominion men tremble and fear before the God of Daniel" (v. 27).

The plot of the story is very similar to that of ch. 3, and is a variant on the folkloric plot of the "Disgrace and Rehabilitation of a Minister." The motif of court conflict shapes this story to a greater degree than the earlier one, since the action is initiated by a conspiracy and the deliverance of Daniel is balanced by the destruction of the conspirators. The traditional plot is given a specifically religious twist by making Daniel's deliverance depend on divine intervention rather than on human initiative. This point is underlined by the inability of the king to save Daniel and his prayer that God do so (v. 16). The analogy with martyr legends recedes, however, since there is no confrontation between Daniel and his accusers or the king. Bentzen has suggested that the story has a biblical point of departure in Ps 57:5-7 (*RSV* 4-6—"I lie in the midst of lions . . .") or 91:13 ("you will tread on the lion and the adder . . ."). These verses at most explain the choice of a lions' den and do not account for the plot of the story, nor do they provide the context for it. While anyone familiar with Scripture could make the association, there is no reason to regard the story as a midrash.

The subordinate forms in Daniel 6 include:

(1) PETITION by the conspirators to the king (vv. 7-9), consisting of a salutation, a statement of what is desired, and a request for an edict. (Cf. the petitions in Esth 3:8-9; 8:5-6; 9:13.)

(2) ACCUSATION (vv. 13-14), consisting of a question to the king, his self-committing answer, and the accusation proper. As in Daniel 3, the force of the accusation depends on an ad hoc decree, of which the king must be reminded. Here the reminder is in the form of a question to the king.

(3) PRAYER OF PETITION (v. 17) on the lips of the king for the deliverance of Daniel.

(4) EPISTLE of Darius (vv. 26-27), marked by the epistolary greeting and containing two other forms:

(5) DECREE OR PROCLAMATION, which is simply stated in v. 27, and

(6) DOXOLOGY, which is a descriptive HYMN OF PRAISE, giving the rationale for the decree.

Setting

The historical problems raised by the ostensible setting have been touched on in connection with the mention of Darius the Mede at the end of the previous unit. The reorganization of the satrapies may reflect the activity of Darius I of Persia, who created twenty satrapies (Herodotus *Hist.* 3.89). The three presidencies, and the super-presidency occupied by Daniel, are not otherwise attested. There is no evidence that a Persian (or Median!) king would have forbidden petitions to any god or man except himself. The folkloric character of the lions' den is shown by its reappearance in the story of Bel and the Dragon.

On the other hand we note that Darius appears throughout to be very well disposed to Daniel and his God. Such a figure can hardly represent Antiochus Epiphanes. The story probably originated in the Hellenistic era, but prior to the time of Epiphanes. The suggestion that all petitions be directed to the king may suggest the divinization of monarchy in the Hellenistic period.

The benign attitude of Darius may, however, be a clue to the social setting of the tale. Problems for Jews in the Diaspora arose from envy and rivalry, but the benevolence of the king is assumed. The author does not wish to question Gentile rule as such. Given the benevolence of the king and the miraculous power of God, any problem can be overcome. We get the impression that the author of this tale was happy with his lot under the Gentile king, found the political status quo satisfactory, and was not eager to change it. We may compare this attitude toward the Greeks with that of much Hellenistic Jewish literature. When the Jews in Alexandria in the first century A.D. were suffering attacks from the Alexandrians, they put the blame on the Egyptians, but tended to exculpate the Greeks, with whom they ultimately wished to be associated (see Josephus *Ag.Ap.* 2.6 §§ 68-70; Philo *Leg. ad Gaium* 166-70; 3 Macc 3:8-10; and J. J. Collins, *Between Athens and Jerusalem: Jewish Identity in the Hellenistic Diaspora* [New York: Crossroad, 1983] 107). This attitude fits well with the interests of upper-class people who hope for advancement within the structures of the society, not by a revolution which might lose what they have already gained.

Intention

The intention of Daniel 6 is summarized succinctly in the royal decree: that all should tremble and fear before the God of Daniel. The story attempts to achieve this effect by arousing wonder, primarily through the miraculous deliverance.

The story also suggests a life-style for Jews in Gentile service. Success at court is not only compatible with fidelity to the Jewish law, but ultimately depends on it. Daniel's religion poses no problem in his service to the king. His excellence is recognized from the start. Problems only arise through the envy of other courtiers, and religion is the occasion that they use. The king is benevolent throughout. As also in Esther, the reader is reassured that the king will appreciate the Jews if he is not misled. There is no objection to Gentile kingship as such. Even when the king is helpless, God can be relied on to rescue those who are blameless before him. There is no suggestion that God will save every Jew in difficulty. Daniel is rescued because of his exceptional piety, but he provides a model that any Jew can imitate.

The martyrs of the Maccabean era did not experience such ready deliverance. Yet the story could obviously lend them reassurance too. The lions' den has a metaphorical quality, like the fiery furnace, which can be applied to any danger. In Christian art and piety the rescue from the lions' den served as an appropriate symbol for the hope of resurrection (Bentzen, *Daniel*, 55).

Bibliography

A. Bentzen, "Daniel 6: Ein Versuch zur Vorgeschichte der Märtyrerlegende," in *Festschrift A. Bertholet* (Tübingen: Mohr, 1950) 58-64.

Chapter 3
The Individual Units:
The Visions

BIBLIOGRAPHY

See Bibliography at " 'Historical' Apocalypses" and "The Book as a Whole."

THE VISION OF THE BEASTS FROM THE SEA AND "SON OF MAN," 7:1-28

Structure

The unity of Daniel 7 has been debated endlessly. The majority of commentators accept the substantial unity of the chapter (Hartman and DiLella are a notable exception). There is, however, a long-standing scholarly tradition, dating from the work of Hölscher and of Noth, which argues for the distinction of different strata. Recent exponents of this view include L. Dequeker, P. Weimar, and R. Kearns. Some scholars, following Hölscher, regard the references to the "little horn" as secondary. Others, following Noth, also bracket vv. 9-10, 13-14 (the visions of the Ancient of Days and "one like a son of man") as redactional.

The source-critical analyses of Daniel 7 are supported by formal considerations: 7:1 has been judged superfluous in view of the first-person introduction to the vision in v. 2. The date formula may belong to the redaction of the entire book, while the long formula "visions of his head as he lay in his bed" recalls Dan 4:13. (Weimar, however, regards 7:1a as a deliberate imitation of the beginning of ch. 2 and only 7:1b as redactional.)

In the vision of the four beasts great weight has been placed on the introductory formulas. The formula "I was seeing . . . and behold" (*ḥzh ḥwyt . . . w'rw; RSV* "I saw . . . and behold") usually introduces the scene, while a second formula "I was seeing until" (*ḥzh ḥwyt 'd dy; RSV* "As I looked") introduces the dynamic action. So the first scene begins (v. 2): "I was seeing in my vision by night, and behold. . . ." Then the sea and the four beasts are introduced and the first beast is described. The second formula follows (v. 4): "I was seeing until its wings were plucked off. . . ." In the second scene, v. 5, the first formula is reduced to "and behold" and the second formula omitted. The third scene, v. 6, has the first formula but not the second. The fourth scene (v. 7), however, echoes the first: "I was seeing in night visions." A symmetrical conclusion is provided by v. 11b: "I was seeing until the beast was slain. . . ."

Verses 8-11a not only interrupt the fourth scene, but also have their own peculiarities. Verse 8 begins: *mśtkl ḥwyt bqrny' w'lw,* "I was considering [*RSV* "I considered"] the horns, and behold." The participle *mśtkl* replaces the otherwise standard *ḥzh* ("seeing"), and the word for "behold" is spelled *'lw* instead of *'rw*. Moreover, the verse introduces an additional "little horn" beyond the schematic number ten. Verse 9, the throne vision, is introduced: "I was seeing until" (*RSV* "As I looked"). The verse is usually printed as poetry (so *RSV*) and regarded as a fragment of an ancient psalm. "I was seeing then . . ." in v. 11a is suspect because of the duplication of the formulaic "I was seeing." If vv. 8-11a, or even just v. 8, are redactional, then the original vision contained no allusion to Antiochus Epiphanes. Since the essay of Haller, many scholars have viewed that original vision as an anti-Hellenistic document from ca. 300 B.C. This reconstruction allows for the existence of an Aramaic book embracing chs. 2-7, prior to the Maccabean era (so, e.g., Steck, 55).

The analysis of the remainder of the chapter depends heavily on the foregoing. The vision of "one like a son of man" in vv. 13-14 is regarded as poetry, like vv. 9-10. Allusions to the "little horn" in the interpretation are necessarily thought to be secondary—so at least vv. 20b, 21-22, 24b-25—but the entire supplementary vision and interpretation (vv. 19-27) and even the initial interpretation (vv. 15-18) are sometimes questioned.

This redaction-critical analysis is open to serious objections, however. It depends heavily on assumptions of original consistency and symmetry. So Kearns (p. 19) posits an ideal structure in the vision of the beasts, wherein each scene contains two parts, introduced by the formulas "I was seeing and behold . . ." and "I was seeing until." He admits that this structure is not consistently realized. In fact, the introductory formulas are marked by persistent variation. This fact casts doubt on arguments which are based on deviation from a supposedly set pattern. (So also Casey.)

The redaction-critical approach to Daniel 7 has not adequately allowed for the use of variation as a stylistic device. This point is most obvious in the discussion of v. 8. That the "little horn" is not integrated into the schematic number ten serves to single it out as an aftergrowth or upstart. The changes in terminology *mśtkl, 'lw*) help further to single out this figure. The variation from *'rw* to *'lw* does not prove redactional activity since both forms were current. A similar variation is found in the Aramaic words for land, *'r''* and *'rq'* in Jer 10:11, within the same sentence. Other examples of such variation are found in the Elephantine papyri. Again, the supplementary vision and interpretation in Dan 7:19-27 separates out the fourth beast and the little horn and makes them the object of special attention. It is, of course, possible that such a passage was added by a redactor, but there is no compelling reason why it could not have been part of the original composition.

The arguments against the authenticity of vv. 9-10 and 13-14 are based primarily on the supposed poetic form of these verses. In the case of vv. 13-14 this characterization is questionable. Niditch has shown that the whole chapter is written in a rhythmic prose style which often comes close to poetry. The classical parallelism which is constitutive of Semitic poetry is lacking in v. 13 and clearly present only in v. 14b. Stylistic considerations do not warrant a distinction between these verses and the rest of the chapter. This is also true of vv. 23-27, which are sometimes presented as poetry. Even vv. 9-10, which are admittedly poetic, are not necessarily from a different source for that reason, given the frequent proximity to poetry of the rhythmic prose style. Further, even if these verses are taken verbatim from an older source they do not necessarily disprove the compositional unity of the chapter. It is generally agreed that the visions of the Ancient of Days and "one like a son of man" draw on traditional material in some form. The question is whether the vision of the four beasts ever existed without these passages.

The traditio-historical background of Daniel 7 has a bearing on this question. Many scholars have accepted the view that the imagery of the chapter is derived ultimately from Canaanite mythology, as exemplified in the Ugaritic myth of Baal's struggle with Yamm (Sea). We do not, of course, have an exact prototype for Daniel 7, but we do have a number of crucial parallels with the extant myth. The juxtaposition of the two heavenly figures of the Ancient of Days and the manlike figure riding on the clouds is most satisfactorily explained as derived from a Canaanite myth in which Baal, who is often called "rider of the clouds," approaches the venerable El (so Emerton, and, with discussion of various other proposals, Colpe). Baal's adversary in one cycle of the Ugaritic myths was Yamm or Sea, who was associated with a dragon and a seven-headed serpent. In Daniel 7 the four beasts come up out of the sea. Their marine origin is not adequately explained by the rather flat interpretation that four kings will arise from the earth. Even OT usage (Pss 74:13-17; 89:10-12 [RSV 9-11]; Isa 51:9-10) suggests that the sea is a symbol of chaos. The beasts from the sea in Daniel are chaos monsters, analogous to the sea dragons and serpents of the myth. Since Baal and Yamm belong to the same traditional mythic complex, the juxtaposition here of the rider of the clouds and the turbulent sea can hardly be an accidental result of redactional activity. See further Collins, *Apocalyptic Vision,* 95-106; and idem, "Apocalyptic Genre and Mythic Allusions in Daniel," *JSOT* 21 (1981) 83-100, for rebuttal of objections.

Even apart from the mythological background, the contrast between the manlike figure on the clouds and the hybrid beasts from the sea seems to be an integral part of the chapter. A vision which only described the four beasts and noted that the fourth was slain would seem strangely truncated, since it would provide no explanation of the slaying and no replacement for the fallen power. Even if we grant that 7:11b is the stylistic complement of 7:7, the insertion of the throne vision and judgment scene prior to the death of the beast is appropriate and even necessary, since the judgment is presupposed when the beast is slain. The hypothesis of an original vision which contained neither the allusions to Antiochus Epiphanes nor the judgment scarcely leaves a purposeful text at all. Daniel 7 in its present form can be understood as a highly purposeful structure. No great confidence can be placed in the hypothetical reconstructions of earlier strata.

Genre

Daniel 7 is a SYMBOLIC DREAM VISION. The circumstances of the revelation are indicated in v. 1. The description of the vision follows in multiple segments marked by introductory formulas. The request for interpretation is found in v. 16. The interpretation follows and the process is repeated in the supplementary vision and interpretation. The concluding sentence gives the visionary's reaction.

The symbols in the vision are mainly allegorical, but the Ancient of Days must be construed realistically within the mythic context. The interpretation of the "one like a son of man" is notoriously debated. Some scholars take the image as an allegorical symbol for the Jewish people (so, recently, Hartman and DiLella, Casey), others as a mythic-realistic symbol for an angel (U. B. Müller, Collins, Zevit, Lacocque, among others; for the arguments see Collins, *Apocalyptic Vision,* 123-52).

The main subgenres in Daniel 7 are the THRONE VISION in vv. 9-10, which has some noteworthy similarities to the throne vision in *1 Enoch* 14. Here the throne vision is part of a DESCRIPTION OF JUDGMENT SCENE, with the enthronement of the heavenly judge, opening of the books, and execution of judgment. The judgment scene further includes the EPIPHANY of a heavenly figure, the "one like a son of man." Finally, the angel's interpretation includes an EX EVENTU PROPHECY, especially in vv. 23-25, with reference to Antiochus Epiphanes.

A different set of form-critical categories has been proposed by R. Kearns, based on his redaction-critical analysis. Kearns distinguishes *apocalyptic vision* as the genre of Dan 7:9-10, 13-14. He finds this genre only in Daniel 7 and in the vision of the man from the sea in 4 Ezra 13 and is therefore using the nomenclature in a uniquely restrictive way. Both visions could more accurately be identified as epiphanies of heavenly figures. The *symbolic dream* is the genre of the original vision of the four beasts in Dan 7:2-7, 11; and the *dream with auditory interpretation* embraces Dan 7:2-28, except for glosses. (Kearns also posits various elaborations of the symbolic dream before the addition of the interpretation.) This genre consists of dream, reaction, request for interpretation, and interpretation, and is therefore very similar to what we have defined as the symbolic dream vision.

The main difference between Kearns's analysis and that presented here lies in his assumption that the symbolic dream represents a distinct stratum, prior to the combination of dream and interpretation. There is no adequate source-critical basis for this assumption. The inclusion of the interpretation is the norm rather than the exception in other apocalyptic books. Formal purity is not a reliable guide to the history of the formation of a text.

Two other proposals which bear on the genre of Daniel 7 should be noted. The first would emphasize the dependence of Daniel 7 on ch. 2 and regard the later chapter as a midrashic adaptation of the earlier one. (So Childs, *Introduction to the Old Testament as Scripture*, 617; Hartman and DiLella, 208.) There can be no doubt that Daniel 7 was indeed influenced by ch. 2 in the conception of a dream vision about four kingdoms. Yet comparatively little of Daniel 7 can be explained from this source. The kingdoms are recast as beasts from the sea, and the visions of the ancient one and the manlike figure evoke mythic prototypes which are not suggested in Daniel 2. In short, the influence of ch. 2 is only one factor among others in Daniel 7.

The second proposal, recently put forward by H. S. Kvanig, sees an Akkadian vision as background for Daniel 7. The vision in question was published by W. von Soden in "Die Unterweltvision eines assyrischen Kronprinzen," *ZA* 43 (1936) 1-31 and is translated in *ANET*, 109-10 as "A Vision of the Netherworld." It dates from the seventh century B.C. Like Daniel 7, the Akkadian text reports a dream vision. Several figures in the dream are hybrid creatures (e.g., the gatekeeper of the netherworld has the head of a lion, human hands, and the feet of a bird). There is a vision of the throne of Nergal, ruler of the netherworld. Kvanig's full argument is not yet available; only a preliminary statement has been published. Yet it would seem that the points of contact between the two visions are slight. Although both are dream visions, they are of different types. Daniel sees a symbolic vision which is interpreted by an angel. The Assyrian visionary experiences a dream journey to the netherworld, and there is no allegorical interpretation. The parallels in imagery are also limited. The Assyrian vision has no counterpart to the great sea or to the manlike figure riding on the clouds. The figure who is brought before the throne for judgment is the visionary himself and he is spared. There is no analogue for the judgment and destruction of the beasts. It seems unlikely then that the Akkadian vision holds the key to either the genre or the symbolism of Daniel 7.

The mythological background of the imagery in Daniel 7 does not determine the genre of the vision, but it does bear on the mode of writing by signaling the affinity of the vision with myth. As noted in the discussion of structure, the primary mythological background of the chapter can be found in the Canaanite myth of Baal's triumph over Yamm (Sea). Compare also Gunkel (pp. 331-35), who pointed to the Babylonian *Enuma Elish* before the Ugaritic texts were discovered. Both the Babylonian and the Ugaritic myths are examples of the pattern of *Chaoskampf* or Combat Myth, in which a hero god triumphs over a chaos monster. While Daniel diverges from the traditional myth in some respects (e.g., the introduction of the judgment scene), it shows a similar pattern. The rider of the clouds triumphs over the monsters from the deep. The protagonists are identified in a new way in Daniel's vision, but the mythic pattern plays a significant role in the effect of the story.

The specific descriptions of the beasts are not drawn from any known variant of the *Chaoskampf*. Perhaps the most popular suggestion has looked to Hos 13:7-8, where God threatens that he will be to Israel like a lion, a leopard, a bear, or a "wild beast." Porter relates the beasts to the "root metaphor" of the shepherd, whereby the nations hostile to Israel are described as wild beasts, as in the nearly contemporary *Animal Apocalypse* of *1 Enoch*. He views the hybrid character of the beasts in the light of Babylonian birth omens, and this suggestion is in accord with the general influence of mantic wisdom on Daniel. Porter's suggestions are compatible with the influence of Hosea 13 and with the use of the *Chaoskampf* as the conceptual frame for the vision. By contrast, the claim that the animal imagery derives from treaty curses (Wittstruck) has only uncertain textual support and is not justified by the context in Daniel (see Rimbach).

Setting

The literary setting of ch. 7 in the book of Daniel is central, not in a strict quantitative sense, although it is close to the midpoint of the book, but in its relations to the other units. It is a transitional chapter, tied to the preceding tales by the use of the Aramaic language and by affinities with ch. 2, but tied to the following visions by its subject matter and by its close parallels with ch. 8. It is also arguably the most elaborate and powerful chapter of the book and so has been regarded with some justification as the heart of Daniel's revelation.

Despite the dating to the reign of Belshazzar, the historical setting of the vision is in the persecution of the Jews by Antiochus Epiphanes that began in 167 B.C. In view of the sequence of kingdoms presupposed throughout the book, the four kingdoms must be identified as Babylonian, Median, Persian, and Greek. Since the fourth beast has ten horns, a date before the third century is unlikely, and no Greek king before Antiochus Epiphanes is known to have inspired such antipathy among Jews. The identification of the "little horn" with a "mouth speaking great things" (7:8) as Epiphanes may be implied already in 1 Macc 1:24 (he "spoke with great arrogance") and is found in Porphyry (Montgomery, 293). It is confirmed by the explicit reference to the persecution in v. 25, where he "shall think to change the times and the law," an allusion to the suppression of the religious festivals (2 Macc 6:6) and of the Torah (1 Macc 1:41-64).

Various attempts have been made to identify the ten horns, especially the three which were uprooted before Epiphanes. The number ten is, of course, schematic. The characterization of Epiphanes as an eleventh makes the point that he is an upstart, whose reign is out of due sequence. Nevertheless, we should expect that there were specific referents for the three uprooted horns. We should note that the text does not say that the eleventh horn uprooted them, and so it is not necessary to suppose that Epiphanes was directly responsible for their removal. Epiphanes was the younger son of Antiochus III the Great. When his father died in 187 B.C. the elder son reigned as Seleucus IV Philopator. Epiphanes, who had been a hostage in Rome, was released in exchange for Seleucus's son Demetrius ca. 176 or early 175 B.C. Then Seleucus died, allegedly murdered by his minister Heliodorus, who seized power, using another son of Seleucus named Antiochus as figurehead. Antiochus Epiphanes then returned and seized power. Thus the three horns were most probably Seleucus, who was uprooted by Heliodorus, and his sons, whose right to succession was usurped. The ten horns could then be filled out as Alexander the Great, Seleucus I, Antiochus I and II, Seleucus II and III, and Antiochus III. (So also Plöger, *Daniel*, 116.) Some scholars dispute whether Alexander should be counted, but we must emphasize that the number ten is schematic in any case. (For the history of Epiphanes' succession see O. Mørkholm, *Antiochus IV of Syria* [Copenhagen: Gyldendalske Boghandel, 1966].)

Daniel 7 was written after the outbreak of the persecution and suppression of the festivals and certainly before the rededication of the temple by Judas Maccabee in 164 B.C., since the duration of the persecution is inaccurately predicted as three and a half years. Since Daniel 7 is written in Aramaic and is reflected in ch. 8, it is generally assumed to be the oldest of the visions, and so was probably written early in the persecution, possibly before the desecration of the temple in December 167, since that event is not clearly reflected here.

The social setting of Daniel 7 is in very sharp contrast to that of ch. 6. Not only is the king in ch. 7 not benevolent; he is a demonic monster. The new perspective is directly the result of the persecution of Antiochus Epiphanes, but it is applied retrospectively to the whole Greek empire and indeed to all the world-empires.

Despite the drastic change in perspective, we must assume that there was continuity between the authors of the tales and those of the visions. Daniel, the supposed visionary, is the main hero of the tales. The visions continue to view Jewish history in the context of the world-empires. The "Danielic circle" must have undergone some changes in the interval, however. Presumably they had returned to Judea from the Diaspora, but we do not know when or why. The change of location may have involved a change of occupation. We will find evidence in ch. 11 that they were teachers. The presumed transition from the Diaspora to Judea may have weakened their attachment to the Gentile kings. Their fortune was no longer to be sought in a foreign court. In ch. 7 the king bears the full brunt of the blame. Daniel 7 does not even refer to the Jewish Hellenizers, although their role will be acknowledged in ch. 11. The problem is seen to lie in the dominion of the Gentile kings. Whereas the tales saw that dominion as ordained by God, ch. 7 presents it as a turbulent revolt.

The offences of Antiochus, highlighted in v. 25, are blasphemy, violence, and religious innovation. Nothing is said of economic matters, at least explicitly. Evidently the people whose point of view is represented by Daniel 7 were religious traditionalists who were directly threatened by the persecution. They still combine religion and politics, but have now a more mystical orientation than is found in the tales. This is illustrated especially in the vision of the divine throne. We must assume that they expected to enjoy power in the universal kingdom, which would be given to the "people of the holy ones," but they say remarkably little about it. Their political aspirations must be qualified in the light of ch. 12, where the primary emphasis is on resurrection and exaltation after death.

The attempt to date an earlier stratum of Daniel 7 as early as 300 B.C. (Noth and others) rests on an uncertain source-critical basis. Besides, there is no evidence of Jewish resistance to Hellenism at that early time.

Intention

The message of Daniel 7 is clearly indicated in the judgment scene when the kingdom is given to the "one like a son of man," or (according to the interpretation) to the holy ones of the Most High or to the people of the holy ones of the Most High. Whether the holy ones are identified as the angelic counterparts of the Jews (Noth, Dequeker, Collins) or only as the Jews themselves (Hartman and DiLella, Casey), this conclusion is evidently a source of comfort in the face of persecution.

This summary of the message of Daniel 7, however, is far from doing justice to the effect of the vision, which is heavily dependent on the symbolism. Initially, the turbulent sea and the monsters which emerge from it inspire terror rather than allay it. The dream does not simply describe the situation of the Jews in the Maccabean period. It construes this situation in a particular light, as a scene of terror. The full force of this vision can only be appreciated if we recognize the allusion to the ancient myth where the sea (Yamm) represented primordial chaos. The terror is then balanced by the sublimity of the throne vision and the judgment. The manlike figure riding on the clouds is in evident contrast to the beasts rising from the sea. The force and significance of the contrast is again enhanced if we recognize the allusion to the ancient myth in which Baal, rider of the clouds, triumphs over Yamm. Daniel is asserting that the struggle in which the Jews are involved is a reenactment of the primordial battle of the myth. The vision conveys at once an understanding of the nature of this struggle and an assurance about its ultimate outcome.

The imagery of the "one like a son of man" and the "holy ones of the Most High" also bears directly on our understanding of the vision. The arguments have often been rehearsed and need not be repeated here. (See Collins, *Apocalyptic Vision*, 123-52.) We shall find throughout Daniel 7–12 that human events are acted out against a backdrop of supernatural, angelic activity. The worldview presupposed is most clearly expressed in chs. 10–12. Indeed, the vision of the beasts from the sea, by its mythological resonance, suggests that Daniel does not see the conflict as merely between human parties. It is very unlikely that the "one like a son of man" and the "holy ones" are mere ciphers for the persecuted Jews. Rather, they are mythic-realistic symbols which refer to the angelic powers, under their leader Michael, which Daniel believed would enable the Jews to prevail.

The function of Daniel 7 is indeed to exhort and console the persecuted Jews, but this function is performed indirectly by presenting a view of the world as the arena of supernatural forces and by looking to a heavenly judgment for the resolution of the conflict. The implications of this worldview for the message of Daniel, and for the conduct to which it exhorts the persecuted Jews, will be seen more clearly in chs. 10–12.

Ultimately the intention of the book of Daniel must be seen to transcend its historical situation. The vision is deliberately presented in symbolic language which never mentions explicitly the historical referents. Consequently, it could be easily reapplied to new historical situations. At the end of the first century the Jewish historian Josephus understood the fourth kingdom as Rome and this interpretation is also reflected in the apocalypse of 4 Ezra (ch. 13) from the same period. The Gospel writers identified the "Son of Man" who would come on the clouds of heaven as Jesus, and the chapter was long understood to refer to the coming of the messiah in both Jewish and Christian traditions (Montgomery, 321). The particular circumstances of the time of Antiochus Epiphanes were assimilated to the pattern of an ancient myth, and so to a type of situation which might recur in history or be projected forward to the end time. The vision expressed a hope for a transcendent judgment, beyond any human situation and beyond the control of any human power.

Bibliography

M. Casey, *Son of Man: The Interpretation and Influence of Daniel 7* (London: SPCK, 1979) 7-50; J. J. Collins, *The Apocalyptic Vision of the Book of Daniel* (HSM 16; Missoula: Scholars Press, 1977) 127-32; idem, "Apocalyptic Genre and Mythic Allusions in Daniel," *JSOT* 21 (1981) 83-100; C. Colpe, "Ho huiós toú anthrópou," *TDNT* 8 (1972) 408-20; J. Coppens, "La chapitre VII de Daniel: Lecture et commentaire," *ETL* 54 (1978) 301-22; M. Delcor, "Les sources du chapitre VII de Daniel," *VT* 18 (1968) 290-312; L. Dequeker, "The 'Saints of the Most High' in Qumran and Daniel," *OTS* 18 (1973) 108-87; J. A. Emerton, "The Origin of the Son of Man Imagery," *JTS* 9 (1958) 225-42; A. J. Ferch, *The Son of Man in Daniel 7* (Berrien Springs: Andrews University Press, 1979); H. L. Ginsberg, *Studies in Daniel* (New York: Jewish Theological Seminary, 1948) 5-23, 63-75; H. Gunkel, *Schöpfung und Chaos in Urzeit und Endzeit* (Göttingen: Vandenhoeck & Ruprecht, 1895); M. Haller, "Das Alter von Daniel 7," *ThStKr* 93 (1921) 83-87; G. Hölscher, "Die Entstehung des Buches Daniel," *ThStKr* 92 (1919) 113-38; R. Kearns, *Vorfragen zur Christologie. II: Überlieferungsgeschichtliche und Rezeptionsgeschichtliche Studie zur Vorgeschichte eines christologischen Hoheitstitels* (Tübingen: Mohr, 1980) 16-51; H. S. Kvanig, "Struktur und Geschichte in Dan 7, 1-14," *ST* 32 (1978) 95-117; idem, "An Akkadian Vision as Background for Daniel 7?" *ST* 35 (1981) 85-89; U. B. Müller, *Messias und Menschensohn in jüdischen Apokalypsen und in der Offenbarung des Johannes* (Gütersloh: Mohn, 1972) 19-24; S. Niditch, *The Symbolic Vision in Biblical Tradition* (HSM 30; Chico: Scholars Press, 1983); M. Noth, "Zur Komposition des Buches Daniel," *ThStKr* 98/99 (1926) 143-63; P. A. Porter, *Metaphors and Monsters: A Literary-critical Study of Daniel 7 and 8* (Lund: Gleerup, 1983); J. A. Rimbach, "Critical Notes: Bears or Bees? Sefire I A 31 and Daniel 7," *JBL* 97 (1978) 565-66; O. H. Steck, "Weltgeschehen und Gottesvolk im Buch Daniel," in *Kirche* (*Fest.* G. Bornkamm; ed. D. Lührmann and G. Strecker; Tübingen: Mohr, 1980) 53-78; P. Weimar, "Daniel 7: Eine Textanalyse," in *Jesus und der Menschensohn* (*Fest.* A. Vögtle; ed. R. Pesch and R. Schnackenburg; Freiburg: Herder, 1975) 11-36; T. Wittstruck, "The Influence of Treaty Curse Imagery on the Beast Imagery of Daniel 7," *JBL* 97 (1978) 100-102; Z. Zevit, "The Structure and Individual Elements of Daniel 7," *ZAW* 80 (1968) 385-96.

THE VISION OF THE RAM AND THE HE-GOAT, 8:1-27

Structure

I. Introduction   1-2
  A. Date   1
  B. Indication of place, introduced by "I saw in
    the vision; and when I saw . . ."   2a

This vision is directly related to the preceding one in ch. 7, to which it apparently refers in v. 1 ("after that which appeared to me at the first"). The vision consists of a series of episodes which show a clear progression. First, the ram magnifies itself. Then the he-goat defeats the ram and magnifies itself. Its great horn is broken but the new little horn magnifies itself even up to the Prince of the host (God). The angelic conversation reports that there is a fixed term for the success of the little horn. This conversation is included in the vision, since the transition to the next section is marked clearly at 8:15 ("When I, Daniel, had seen the vision . . ."). The epiphany of the revealer underlines the supernatural authority of the interpretation. The angel passes lightly over the ram and the original goat but repeats the career of the "little horn" in some detail, including his climactic revolt against "the Prince of princes." The interpretation adds a statement which has no counterpart in the vision: "by no (human) hand, he shall be broken." The angel concludes by affirming the reliability of the vision. The concluding statement that Daniel did not understand the vision leaves the door open for further complementary revelations.

It is clear from the interpretation that the climax of the chapter is the revolt of the "little horn" and his ultimate defeat. The duration of the profanation of the temple is highlighted in the angelic conversation, but it appears parenthetical to the vision's main concern with the career of the little horn.

The unity of Daniel 8, like ch. 7, has been contested. The opening verses repeat the words "vision" and "saw" excessively. Some of the repetition may be due to errors in transmission; some of the phrases are not found in the Greek translations.

More substantive disputes have centered on vv. 11-14, where the angelic dialogue has been thought to disrupt the vision. In some cases the argument has been based on content (e.g., Hartman and DiLella maintain that "in the basic apocalypse the 'holy ones' are the pious Jews," whereas they are undeniably angels in these verses; this argument collapses if the "holy ones" are angels throughout). Other arguments are based on form (Hasslberger): the verb form switches from feminine (in agreement with horn) to masculine (anticipating the interpretation), and the "holy ones" are mythic-realistic figures unlike the allegorical symbols of the ram and the goat. The change in verb form shows that the author did not maintain his allegory consistently, but such a slip does not require us to posit a second writer. There is no reason why one vision cannot contain both allegorical and mythic-realistic symbols; both are also found in Daniel 7. The objections to the authenticity of these verses, then, cannot be sustained. Verse 26a, which refers to "the vision of the evenings and the mornings," stands or falls with the angelic dialogue to which it refers.

A question has been raised about v. 16 because it uses the word *mar'eh* for vision, instead of the more usual *ḥāzôn* (Ginsberg, *Studies*, 29-38), and also because Daniel's vision had ended in v. 15 (Hartman and DiLella). The latter point can carry no weight—there is no reason why Daniel should not have had further visions after v. 15. And the change in terminology is not an adequate justification for textual surgery.

There is apparent duplication between vv. 17 and 18-19—Daniel is twice said to fall prostrate and the angel twice explains that the vision refers to the end. The redundancy serves some formal purpose; the first formulation rounds out the epiphany, while the second introduces the interpretation. It may be, however, that the duplication results from conflation of different textual readings. There is no evidence of purposeful redactional alteration. (The argument of Hartman and DiLella that *qēṣ* is eschatological in v. 17 but not in v. 19 is unfounded.)

Finally, Hasslberger and Hartman and DiLella object that the concluding statement that Daniel did not understand the vision is incompatible with the fact that the angel has explained it. Unfortunately Daniel was not the last person to remain bewildered by this vision after an explanation had been given!

Genre

The vision in Daniel 8 is not explicitly said to be a dream, but it conforms to the pattern of the SYMBOLIC DREAM VISION. Daniel's presence in Susa should be understood as a transportation in the spirit ("and when I saw, I was in Susa"; cf. the transportation of Ezekiel in Ezekiel 8), despite the claim of Josephus that he was physically there (Josephus *Ant.* 10.11.7 §§263-66). The chapter exhibits the full pattern of the genre:

—indication of circumstances
—description of the vision, introduced by "behold"
—request (or desire) for interpretation
—interpretation and
—concluding material.

As we have noted, the vision uses both allegorical and mythic-realistic symbols. The most distinctive variation on the pattern here is the EPIPHANY of the interpreting angel. This feature links Daniel 8 not only to the more elaborate epiphany in Daniel 10 but also to Ezekiel 8.

Daniel 8:23-25 has been identified as an example of REGNAL or dynastic PROPHECY, analogous to the Babylonian Dynastic Prophecy (so Grayson, 21). A more extensive example of this genre will be found in ch. 11.

Daniel 8 is clearly influenced by a number of biblical models. Most obviously it is a companion piece for Daniel 7 ("that which appeared to me at the first," 8:1). Daniel 7 is the model for the form of the symbolic vision. It is not followed rigidly, but it supplies some of the crucial symbolism, especially the "little horn" and the use of "holy ones" for angels. It may well be that chs. 7 and 8 were written by different persons, in view of the transition from Aramaic to Hebrew and the stylistic differences between the chapters. (See Niditch, ch. 3: Daniel 8 uses brief clauses, in contrast to the chains of synonymous terms characteristic of Daniel 7.) Yet Daniel 8 is evidently designed to complement ch. 7 and shares the same conceptual and symbolic world. Together they are parts of a composite whole. If that whole was produced by a group rather than by an individual it is nonetheless a coherent literary work.

A second biblical model operative in Daniel 8 is found in the book of Ezekiel. Daniel's location by a river recalls Ezek 1:1. The apparition of a figure in human likeness recalls Ezek 8:2 (LXX; MT must be emended from '*ēš*, "fire," to '*îš*, "man"). The manner of address, *ben 'ādām* ("son of man"), is also derived from Ezekiel. The model of Ezekiel applies most directly to the epiphany of the angel.

A third biblical influence is evident in the echoes of Habakkuk in 8:17, 19. Hab 2:3 reads *kî 'ôd ḥāzôn lammô'ēd wĕyāpēaḥ laqqēṣ wĕlō' yĕkazzēb* ("For still the vision awaits its time; it hastens to the end—it will not lie"). Daniel 8:17, 19 play on the terms *ḥāzôn, mô'ēd,* and *qēṣ* to suggest that the vision is for "the time of the end" and that the end will come in its appointed time. The eschatological reading of Habakkuk presupposed in Daniel finds a parallel now in the famous pesher on Habakkuk from Qumran.

The use of biblical models does not in itself make Daniel 8 either a MIDRASH or a PESHER. Other models are operative besides. Porter's observation of the use of animal imagery for Gentile nations is relevant here, but does not explain the specific choice of animals. It is now generally acknowledged that the symbolism of the ram and the he-goat is astrological and refers to the constellations thought in the Hellenistic age to preside over Persia and Syria (Caquot, Koch). The rise of the little horn, which casts some of the stars to the ground, recalls the allusion to Helal ben Shachar ("Lucifer [*RSV* Daystar], son of Dawn") in Isa 14:12. This in turn presupposes a MYTH which is not fully articulated in the Bible, and which may be ultimately related to the Ugaritic story of Attar's attempt to occupy the throne of Baal. This myth provides the paradigm for a crucial element of Daniel's vision, the hybris of the little horn and the assurance that it will be broken. Daniel 8, however, fashions a new whole from its various models. In no case can it be said to exist for the sake of explaining any of its prototypes.

Setting

The dating to the reign of Belshazzar is a transparent fiction. The ram and the he-goat are interpreted explicitly as the kings of Media-Persia and Greece. The goat's first horn, which is broken, is clearly Alexander the Great, and the four horns which rise in its place are the generals who succeeded him. There is no doubt that the little horn is Antiochus Epiphanes, not only because the symbol is repeated from Daniel 7 but also because of what he does. The key to the historical setting lies in the information that the continual burnt offering was taken away and the place of the sanctuary overthrown. This is a clear reference to the desecration of the Jerusalem temple in December 167 B.C. The chapter was probably written shortly after that event. It must also have been composed soon after Daniel 7, since that chapter was written after the outbreak of the persecution in mid-167 B.C.

Some scholars have suggested that the vision of the ram and the he-goat originally focused on the overthrow of the Persian empire by Alexander the Great (e.g., Hasslberger, 401). The astrological symbolism, however, would be difficult to explain on that hypothesis, since the goat is associated with Syria rather than with Greece. Even if the hypothesis were correct, it would only concern approximately Dan 8:3-7, and we could not be sure of the original extent or purpose of the composition.

This vision introduces two matters which may be significant for the social location of the author and his circle. One is the intense concern for the desecrated sanctuary. This concern has suggested to some the hypothesis that the book originated in priestly circles (Lebram). Yet this inference is by no means necessary. Pious scribes in Jerusalem could equally well have felt the distress expressed here. Although the desecration of the temple is singled out in the angelic dialogue, it is not the ultimate focus of the vision. Rather, as in Daniel 7, the final concern is with the problem of Gentile power and world sovereignty.

The second matter introduced here is more informative about the social location. The little horn will not be broken by human hands. The author, then, is scarcely a supporter of the Maccabean revolt. His reliance on supernatural power will be evident again in ch. 11, and its implications will be more fully developed there.

Intention

The primary purpose of this chapter is surely to suggest that the career of Antiochus conforms to the Lucifer pattern: hybris leads to a great fall. The chapter gradually builds up to the climax in v. 25. The vision begins with the ram which "did as he pleased and magnified himself" (v. 4). Yet when the he-goat appears the ram has no power to resist. Then the he-goat "magnified himself exceedingly; but when he was strong, the great horn was broken." The little horn, then, appears as the last in a series. It "grew great, even to the host of heaven" and "magnified itself, even up to the Prince of the host"; i.e., it exalted itself more than any of its predecessors. At this point the fulfillment of the pattern is delayed, first by the angelic dialogue, then by the epiphany of the interpreter. The interpretation repeats the account of Antiochus's rise, until "he shall even rise up against the Prince of princes." The conclusion is inevitable, and is stated with terse finality: "by no human hand, he shall be broken." This pattern of the rise and fall of human kingdoms runs throughout the book of Daniel, from ch. 2 on. It will be evident again in ch. 11.

The angelic dialogue with which the vision concludes introduces an important subsidiary concern, "for how long is the vision?" (v. 13). This question is highlighted by its position at the end of the vision, by the transition from vision to audition, and by the fact that it is expressed as a dialogue between angels. Most important is the assurance that the time is measured out and its duration is determined. The actual figure given, 1,150 days, will be subject to revision later in the book. The preservation of different figures side by side (most conspicuously in 12:11, 12) suggests that the assurance that the end would come at an appointed time was more important than any specific date that could be given. Both the pattern and the prediction, then, serve the purpose of consolation in the face of the persecution.

Bibliography

A. Caquot, "Sur les quatre Bêtes de Daniel VII," *Sem* 5 (1955) 5-13; A. Grayson, *Babylonian Historical-Literary Texts* (Toronto: University of Toronto Press, 1975); B. Hasslberger, *Hoffnung in der Bedrängnis* (St. Ottilien: Eos Verlag, 1977) 1-110; K. Koch, "Vom profetischen zum apokalyptischen Visionsbericht," in *Apocalypticism in the Mediterranean World and the Near East* (ed. D. Hellholm; Tübingen: Mohr, 1983) 413-46; S. Niditch, *The Symbolic Vision in Biblical Tradition* (HSM 30; Chico: Scholars Press, 1983); P. Porter, *Metaphors and Monsters: A Literary-critical Study of Daniel 7 and 8* (Lund: Gleerup, 1983).

THE INTERPRETATION OF JEREMIAH'S PROPHECY, 9:1-27

Structure

I. Introduction	1-2
A. Date: first year of Darius	1
B. Occasion: reading of Jeremiah's prophecy	2
II. Daniel's prayer	3-19
A. Introductory statement	3-4a
B. The prayer	4b-19
1. Invocation	4b
2. Confession of sin	5-11a
a. Direct confession of sin	5-6
b. Confession combined with acknowledgment of divine justice	7-8
c. Confession in terms of breach of covenant	9-11a
3. Description of divine punishment (marked by switch to passive verb in 11b)	11b-14
a. Affirmation that the covenantal curses have been fulfilled	11b-13
b. Affirmation of God's justice	14
4. Prayer for mercy	15-19
a. Invocation, introduced by "and now"	15a
b. Reminder of Exodus	15b
c. Confession of sin	15c
d. Fourfold supplication, each consisting of request plus reason ("for thy own sake")	16-19
III. The revelation	20-27
A. Introductory statement of circumstances	20-21a
B. Epiphany of angel	21b

The main issue in dispute concerns the authenticity of the prayer in vv. 3-19. The Hebrew style of the prayer contrasts sharply with that of the rest of Daniel 8–12: it is a smoothly flowing pastiche of traditional phrases, free from Aramaisms. The dispute, however, is not about the authorship of the prayer, since the author of Daniel could have incorporated a traditional prayer and made it part of his composition (so, e.g., Montgomery). The argument is that the prayer is a secondary addition, after the completion of the book. It depends on two factors: First, the beginning and end of the prayer are marked by duplications (vv. 3, 4a, and 20, 21a), which have been taken as redactional seams. Second, many scholars have argued that the prayer is incongruous in its context. We should expect the prayer of an individual for illumination as in 4 Ezra 12:7-9. Instead we find a communal confession of sin. (Scholars who reject the prayer on these grounds include Ginsberg, Bentzen, and Hartman and DiLella. The arguments were formulated by A. von Gall in his dissertation, "Die Einheitlichkeit des Buches Daniel" [Giessen: Ricker, 1895].)

On the other hand, B. W. Jones has pointed out that "several words of the prayer are repeated in the conclusion of the chapter, or are recalled in some way" (p. 491): *lhśkyl* in vv. 13 and 22; forms of *šûb* and *śkl* in vv. 13 and 25; a form of *šmm* occurs in v. 17 apropos of the desolation of the temple, and again in v. 27 (the abomination of desolation); and there is a play on the word *šōmĕmōtênû* in v. 18; in v. 11 an oath *(šbʻh)* is poured out *(tittak)* on the Jews, in v. 24 the weeks *(šbʻîm)* are decreed *(nehtak)*, and in v. 27 the decreed end is poured out *(tittak)*. Moreover, both the prayer and its framework refer to Jerusalem, which otherwise appears in Daniel only in 1:1. The word for supplications *(thnwnym)* appears in Daniel only in ch. 9, but in both prayer and framework. Words of the root *hṭ'* ("sin") appear in the prayer and in vv. 20 and 24 (framework), but otherwise only in Dan 4:24 (Gilbert, 291).

Whether the prayer is incongruous in its context is disputed. According to v. 3, Daniel turns to the Lord with fasting, sackcloth, and ashes. Fasting is often a preparation for receiving a revelation (so Daniel 10 and 4 Ezra, repeatedly). The sackcloth and ashes are penitential garb, however, and suggest that Daniel 9 is influenced by penitential liturgies (Lipinski, Gilbert). Despite the usual assumptions of commentators, Daniel does not ask for enlightenment about the "seventy years" of Jeremiah, or even express bewilderment about it. His reaction to the prophecy is not puzzlement but distress. Accordingly we should not necessarily assume that a prayer for enlightenment was implied here. The traditional confession of sin and prayer for mercy is an appropriate reaction to the prophecy of Jeremiah. That Daniel prays in the plural is explicable if he is understood to pray on behalf of the people (cf. the prayer of Ezra in Ezra 9).

Another incongruity remains, however. The prayer is heavily Deuteronomic in its theology. It implies that the Jews are being punished for their sins and that God may relent if they do penance. The remainder of Daniel, including the angel's prophecy, views the course of history as predetermined because of the conduct of the Jews and not subject to alteration. The apparent contradiction between the theology of the prayer and that of the rest of the book is perhaps the major problem posed by this chapter (see Intention below). On strictly literary grounds, however, the apparent evidence for redactional seams must be weighed against the linguistic correspondences noted by Jones and Gilbert that suggest that the conclusion was written with the prayer in view. We have found some duplication also in the introductions to chs. 7 and 8. It is possible that such redundancy is simply a feature of the author's style and not necessarily indicative of redactional activity. While the matter is not beyond doubt, I am now inclined to reverse my earlier opinion (*Apocalyptic Vision*, 185-87) and accept the view that the traditional prayer was included by the author of Daniel 9 rather than by a later redactor.

The structure of the angel's prophecy requires some further comment. While it contains some rhythmic passages, the prophecy as a whole cannot be construed as poetry (pace Shea), but it achieves symmetry by balancing contrasts. The first major point of transition comes at the end of seven weeks, with the coming of a *mšyḥ ngyd* ("anointed prince"—Zerubbabel or Joshua the high priest) and the rebuilding of Jerusalem. Then all is well, though times are hard, for sixty-two weeks. The second point of transition comes then, when a *mšyḥ* ("anointed one") is cut off and Jerusalem is destroyed. The *nāgîd* ("prince") who comes at this point is destructive. He undoes the sacrificial cult, whose restoration was promised at the beginning of the prophecy. The prophecy concludes with a promise that he will be destroyed. The middle period of sixty-two weeks is regarded as a relatively satisfactory time, and there is a measure of correspondence between the *Urzeit* of the Exile and the *Endzeit* when the cult is again disrupted.

Genre

The dominant genre of Daniel 9 is the ANGELIC DISCOURSE. The PRAYER, which expresses Daniel's distress, and the EPIPHANY of the angel can be viewed as introductory material for the revelation.

The discourse itself is an exegetical MIDRASH or PESHER on Jer 25:11-12; 29:10. The angel does not explicitly claim to be expounding Jeremiah's prophecy, but the association is obvious in view of Daniel's preoccupation in 9:2.

The content of the midrash is an EX EVENTU PROPHECY in periodized form. The particular schema of seventy weeks of years is most probably suggested by the system of sabbatical years in Leviticus 25, which stipulated a jubilee after seven weeks of years. (Cf. also Lev 26:18, where God threatens to punish the disobedient sevenfold.) Klaus Koch has suggested that the number was extrapolated from the historical books of the Bible. The period from the Exodus to the building of the temple is reckoned at 480 years (1 Kgs 6:1). From then to its destruction was 430 years and the Exile was supposed to last seventy years (Jeremiah; Zech 1:12). Therefore the total time from the Exodus to the restoration was 980 years (or twice 490). The period from Abraham to Sinai is also about 490 years, if allowance is made for Abraham's sojourn in Canaan. Koch suggests an underlying idea of a world-year with seven epochs of 490 years each. It must be said that the evidence for this view is not precise, but Koch may be on the right track in positing apocalyptic speculation on the duration of the world. Parallels to Daniel 9 are found in several apocalyptic writings of the second century B.C., most notably in the *Apocalypse of Weeks* in *1 Enoch* 93, where the turning point of history comes at the end of the seventh week. In the *Animal Apocalypse* (*1 Enoch* 83–90) Israel is subjected to seventy shepherds. *T. Levi* 16:1 says that the priesthood will be profaned for seventy weeks, and claims to derive this knowledge from the book of *Enoch.* The Melchizedek Scroll from Qumran (11QMelch) has a schema of ten jubilees or 490 years, and there the background in Leviticus is obvious. The schema of seventy weeks is also explicit in the Pesher on the Periods (4Q180 and 181) from Qumran (J. T. Milik, *The Books of Enoch* [Oxford: Oxford University Press, 1976] 249–53).

Daniel's schema need not have been an ad hoc exegesis of Jeremiah, but may have been a deliberate conjunction of Jeremiah's prophecy and an apocalyptic schema which had been developed independently.

The PRAYER in Daniel 9 is a COMMUNAL CONFESSION OF SIN and a PETITION for mercy, like the Prayer of Azariah (see Gunkel, Westermann). Other major examples are found in Psalm 106; Ezra 9:6-15; Neh 1:5-11; 9:5-37; the "Words of the Luminaries" from Qumran; and Bar 1:15–3:8. (See further Steck, *Israel,* 110-36.) All these prayers are closely related to the so-called covenant form. They typically involve: 1) confession of breach of covenant, 2) admission of God's righteousness, 3) recollection of God's mercies, and 4) appeal for mercy for God's own sake.

The EPIPHANY of the angel is not developed here. It is simply a statement of the angel's arrival, without an accompanying description.

Setting

The fictional setting of Daniel 9 is in the first year of Darius the Mede, presumably the first year after the fall of Babylon, so 539/38 B.C., considerably less than seventy years after the fall of Jerusalem. The actual historical setting must be inferred from the *ex eventu* prophecy. The latest events mentioned are the disruption of the sacrificial cult and the introduction of the "abomination of desolation" into the Jerusalem temple. We may infer that the chapter was written shortly after these events, at the end of 167 or very early in 166 B.C.

Daniel's reinterpretation of Jeremiah's seventy years contrasts with other interpretations in the postexilic period. 2 Chr 36:20-21 saw the fulfillment of the prophecy in the restoration under Cyrus (after less than fifty years). Zech 1:12 related it to the restoration of the temple (which was roughly accurate). Daniel extends the period of the "desolations of Jerusalem" enormously. The implied evaluation of the postexilic period is important for Daniel's location in the Judaism of the time. On the one hand, he can scarcely have belonged to the ruling priestly class, whose viewpoint is represented by books like Chronicles and Zechariah. This conclusion is not invalidated by the prominence of priestly and cultic terminology in 9:24, the sympathy for the "anointed one" who is cut off (presumably

Onias III), or the probable Levitical background of the seventy weeks of years. Daniel 9 is the only passage in the book where cultic motifs are prominent. Concern for the violated temple cult, however, must have been shared by many Jews outside priestly circles. On the other hand, Daniel's attitude to the postexilic period is not as negative as what we find in some other apocalyptic writings. The *Apocalypse of Weeks* in *1 Enoch* 93 ignores the restoration and refers only to "an apostate generation." The *Animal Apocalypse* (*1 Enoch* 89:73) implies that all the offerings in the second temple were unclean. *Testament of Levi* 16 also implies widespread cultic corruption in the postexilic period. By contrast, Daniel suggests that the sixty-two weeks after the restoration will be relatively satisfactory. Daniel is certainly in no way alienated from the temple cult. The circle which produced Daniel, then, should be distinguished from the priests who had ruled Judea for most of the postexilic period, on the one hand, and from the group that produced the *Enoch* literature, on the other.

As noted above, it is probable that Daniel's prayer is a traditional piece which was not originally composed for its present setting. If this is so, it could have been composed at any time after the Exile. It is not necessary to insist on a setting in the actual Exile (so Lacocque). We may infer from the number and diffusion of similar prayers that there was an ongoing synagogal tradition down into the Hellenistic period (see Steck, *Israel*).

The inclusion of this prayer tells us little about the author's circle. Any observant Jew would have been familiar with the liturgical tradition. We cannot affiliate everyone who used such a prayer with the Hasidim, especially since we have virtually no explicit information about the theology of that group. The inclusion of the prayer does, however, weigh against any suggestion that Daniel was produced by a narrowly sectarian group.

The lack of Aramaisms is not significant because of the conservative character of liturgical language. The significant setting of this prayer, before its incorporation into Daniel, is not the uncertain time or place of its composition but the liturgical tradition which persisted for centuries and was strongly Deuteronomic in inspiration.

Intention

The primary intention of Daniel 9 is to assure the persecuted Jews that the time of trial is coming to an end by locating it in an overview of history. This is achieved through the angel's revelation, which specifies the total duration of the postexilic period (from "the going forth of the word to restore and rebuild Jerusalem"). The profanation of the temple is to last for half a week (i.e., three and a half years, or a time, two times, and half a time). The attention to specific lengths of time is significant for its psychological effect and was noted in antiquity as a distinctive characteristic of Daniel's prophecy (Josephus *Ant.* 10.11.7 §267).

Two other issues bear on the finer nuances of the intention of the chapter. One is the function of the prayer, and the other is the understanding of history in vv. 24-27. These two issues are directly related to each other.

We have noted already that the prayer has a strongly Deuteronomic character which contrasts, in the view of most scholars, with the theology of Daniel, including that expressed in 9:24-27. One solution to this anomaly is to suppose that the prayer was added by a redactor whose theology differed from that of the apocalyptic book. If we accept the view that the prayer was included, though not composed, by the author of the revelation, various possibilities arise.

B. W. Jones has argued that the prayer is placed here deliberately to contrast with the angel's interpretation. "The prayer is needed to 'set the stage' for Gabriel, and when the prayer is ignored we are being told, in effect, that the calamity was decreed and will end at the appointed time, quite apart from prayers, and quite apart from previous ideas of retribution" (Jones, 493).

In a somewhat different vein W. S. Towner argues that the prayer is not intended to influence the will of God but is an act of piety in itself, a *miṣwâ*: "It is, taken as a whole, an illustration of the activity of a faithful man living between the times, testifying to his utter dependence upon a God of righteousness and *ḥesed* and celebrating the manifest greatness of such a God" (Towner, 213).

On the other hand, O. H. Steck has argued for a more integral relation between the prayer and its context, by discerning a Deuteronomic view of history in 9:24-27 (Steck, "Weltgeschehen," 65-75). For Steck, the crucial idea is that the sufferings of the Jews are seen as a punishment for sin. This idea is first introduced in Daniel in 8:19, where the "indignation" *(za'am)* which must come to an end is understood as the punitive wrath of God. In ch. 9 this understanding of history emerges more clearly. The duration of the seventy weeks of years is decreed "to finish the transgression, to put an end to sin [reading *hātēm* for *ḥᵃtōm*] and to atone for iniquity" (so also Janssen and Zimmerli). Steck contrasts the focus on the history of Israel in ch. 9 with the concern for the world-kingdoms in chs. 7 and 8. He argues then that Daniel 9 attests a shift in the theology of the book and ascribes it to the influence of the Deuteronomic strand of tradition, which we find in the penitential prayers of the postexilic period.

Steck's interpretation is open to question at several points. If Daniel now wishes to explain the distress of the Jews as a punishment for their sins, it is remarkable that the angel never says so explicitly, e.g., that the seventy weeks of years are decreed because of the sin of the people. The data from which Steck's interpretation is inferred are actually quite ambiguous.

Daniel 9:24 states that the seventy weeks of years are decreed "to finish the transgression, to put an end to sin, and to atone for iniquity, to bring in everlasting righteousness, to seal [i.e., validate] both vision and prophet, and to anoint a most holy place." These infinitives evidently refer to the end of the time period. The focal point is the rededication of the temple. This event, and the decreed end which is to be poured out on the desolator (9:27), will mark the end of sin and the coming of eternal righteousness. "To atone for iniquity," then, is not an ongoing process for the seventy weeks of years, but something that will happen at the end and apparently will coincide with the rededication of the temple. The sin and iniquity are not specified, but they surely include the desecration of the temple by the Syrians and the Hellenizers. The complexity of this question becomes apparent in ch. 11, where a clear distinction is drawn between the righteous and sinners within the Jewish people. The traditional Deuteronomic idea of the sins of Israel, which is presupposed in the prayer, is not adequately nuanced for the situation envisaged by 9:24.

The term *za'am* is used in Dan 8:19 and 11:36, and the verb *zā'am* is used in Zech 1:12, where God is said to have been indignant against Jerusalem for seventy years. Daniel 8 is thus seen to prepare for Daniel 9 by positing an age of wrath which will last until "many days hence" (8:26; Steck, "Weltgeschehen," 67). Common terminology, however, does not necessarily ensure the same understanding. Daniel obviously diverges from Zechariah's understanding of the seventy years. Moreover, the term za'am is not used in Daniel 9 in relation to the seventy weeks of years. In Daniel 8 and 11 it is used with reference to the career of Antiochus Epiphanes, and there it is used absolutely ("the wrath," not, e.g., "the wrath of God") in a way that suggests that it is a quasi-technical term for eschatological woes (cf. already Isa 26:20 and the use of the Greek $org\bar{e}$ in Matt 3:7). Moreover, in Dan 11:30 the verb $z\bar{a}'am$ is used with Antiochus, not God, as subject, which raises the possibility that za'am in 8:19 and 11:36 is the indignation of the king rather than of God. The inference that the whole postexilic period is an age of wrath is scarcely warranted. If Antiochus Epiphanes is seen as an agent of divine wrath (Steck, "Weltgeschehen," 71; cf. Isa 10:5, where za'am [RSV "fury"] is used) this is implicit rather than explicit in the text.

In fact, the angelic revelation in Daniel 9 does not address the question *why* the Jews must endure the desolation of Jerusalem. It is rather concerned with the duration of that desolation. Other Jewish texts from the Hellenistic period do indeed view the persecution as a punishment for sin (2 Macc 7:18; *T. Moses* 8:1; 9:2). If such an understanding is presupposed in Daniel, it is not clearly articulated and is certainly not emphasized. We will find in ch. 11 that the suffering of the righteous Jews is viewed as purificatory (11:35), but this is rather different from the punitive understanding which Steck attributes to the prayer in Daniel 9.

The focus on the history of Israel in Daniel 9 provides a different perspective from the world-kingdoms of Daniel 7 and 8, but the two viewpoints are complementary and there is no necessary tension between them. Even Zech 1:12-17, which clearly sees the seventy years as a punishment for Israel's sins, lays the greater blame on the Gentiles who furthered the disaster. In Daniel, too, the primary cause of the desolation is not the sin of Israel but the rebellious actions of the Gentiles. The protagonist in the last week is Antiochus Epiphanes, not the Jewish Hellenizers, and he is not called the rod of Yahweh's anger by Gabriel in Daniel 9, but is labeled "the desolator."

Moreover, Steck's attempt to assimilate Daniel to the Deuteronomic tradition loses sight of a crucial difference between the theologies of history implied in the prayer and in the angel's discourse, a difference which has been well demonstrated by Jones. The prayer, like the entire Deuteronomic tradition, assumes a causal connection between the people's repentance and supplication and the divine deliverance: the intended sequence is clearly stated in Dan 9:19: "O Lord, hear; O Lord, forgive; O Lord, give heed and act" (cf. Ps 107:13: "Then they cried to the Lord in their trouble, and he delivered them from their distress"). The deliverance promised by the angel, however, is in no sense a response to Daniel's prayer. It will not even come for almost five hundred years; moreover, the word went forth at the *beginning* of Daniel's supplication. The end will come at the appointed time because it is decreed, not because of Daniel's prayer or any act of repentance by the people. This deterministic, apocalyptic view of history is in fundamental contrast to the Deuteronomic theology of the prayer. (This is also true of other apocalyptic texts which Steck assimilates to the Deuteronomic tradition: *Apocalypse of Weeks, Animal Apocalypse, Jubilees* [Steck, *Israel*, 153-62].)

95

What then is the function of the prayer in Daniel 9? As Towner has argued, the prayer is a traditional set piece, and its recitation is an act of piety. While its content does not represent the angel's or the author's theology, it is appropriate as the prayer of one who, at the end of ch. 8, does not understand. We may compare 4 Ezra 8:48-49, where the angel commends Ezra "because you have humbled yourself, as is becoming for you, and have not deemed yourself to be among the righteous." The interpretation proposed by Jones also has merit, since the wisdom imparted to Daniel is indeed a sharp departure from the traditional theology. The conflict of theologies is not as sharp here as in 4 Ezra. We need not assume any polemical intent on the part of the author. In effect, however, Daniel 9 entails a rejection of Deuteronomic theology, not an acceptance of its influence.

Bibliography

J. Doukhan, "The Seventy Weeks of Daniel 9: An Exegetical Study," *AUSS* 17 (1979) 1-22; M. Gilbert, "La Prière de Daniel," *RTL* 3 (1972) 284-310; P. Grelot, "Soixante-dix semaines d'années," *Bib* 50 (1969) 169-86; H. Gunkel and J. Begrich, *Einleitung in die Psalmen* (*HKAT* 1/1; Göttingen: Vandenhoeck & Ruprecht, 1933) 117-39; L. Hartman, "The Functions of Some So-Called Apocalyptic Timetables," *NTS* 22 (1976) 1-14; E. Janssen, *Das Gottesvolk und seine Geschichte* (Neukirchen-Vluyn: Neukirchener, 1971); B. W. Jones, "The Prayer in Daniel ix," *VT* 18 (1968) 488-93; K. Koch, "Die mysteriösen Zahlen der judäischen Könige und die apokalyptischen Jahrwochen," *VT* 28 (1978) 433-41; A. Lacocque, "The Liturgical Prayer in Daniel 9," *HUCA* 47 (1976) 119-42; E. Lipinski, *La Liturgie Penitentielle* (LD 52; Paris: Cerf, 1969) 35-41; C. A. Moore, "Toward the Dating of the Book of Baruch," *CBQ* 26 (1974) 312-20; O. Plöger, " 'Siebzig Jahre,' " *Festschrift Friedrich Baumgärtel* (ed. L. Rost; Erlangen: Universitätsbund Erlangen, 1959) 124-30; W. H. Shea, "Poetic Relations in the Time Periods in Dan 9:25," *AUSS* 18 (1980) 59-63; O. H. Steck, *Israel und das gewaltsame Geschick der Propheten* (WMANT 23; Neukirchen-Vluyn: Neukirchener, 1967); idem, "Weltgeschehen und Gottesvolk im Buch Daniel," in *Kirche* (*Fest.* G. Bornkamm; ed. D. Lührmann and G. Strecker; Tübingen: Mohr, 1980) 53-78; W. S. Towner, "Retributional Theology in the Apocalyptic Setting," *USQR* 26 (1971) 203-14; C. Westermann, "Struktur und Geschichte der Klage im Alten Testament," *ZAW* 66 (1954) 44-80; W. Zimmerli, "Alttestamentliche Prophetie und Apokalyptik auf dem Wege zur 'Rechtfertigung des Gottlosen,' " in *Rechtfertigung* (*Fest.* Ernst Käsemann; ed. J. Friedrich, W. Pöhlmann, and P. Stuhlmacher; Tübingen: Mohr; Göttingen: Vandenhoeck & Ruprecht, 1976) 575-92.

THE ANGEL'S REVELATION, 10:1 – 12:13

Structure

I. Introduction (in third person)	10:1
A. Date formula	1a
B. Summary statements	1b
II. Epiphany of the angel	10:2-9
A. Introduction (in first person)	2-4
1. Preparation of seer	2-3
2. Occasion of vision	4

    B. Description of the epiphany ("I lifted my
       eyes . . . and behold")   5-6
    C. Reactions to the epiphany   7-9
      1. Flight of those who did not see the vision   7
      2. Daniel's reaction to the vision   8
      3. Daniel's reaction to the audition   9
III. Dialogue with the angel (introduced by "and
    behold . . .")   10:10–11:1
    A. Explanatory address by angel   10:10-14
      1. Partial elevation of Daniel   10
      2. Brief address of angel   11a
      3. Rise of Daniel to standing position   11b
      4. Longer address of angel   12-14
    B. Daniel's profession of weakness   10:15-17
      1. Daniel's dumbness   15
      2. Opening of Daniel's mouth   16a
      3. His profession of weakness   16b-17
    C. Angel's reassurance   10:18-19a
      1. By touch   18
      2. By word   19a
    D. Statement by Daniel: "let my lord speak
      . . ."   10:19b
    E. Further explanatory remarks by angel   10:20–11:1
IV. Angelic discourse   11:2–12:4
    A. Introductory statement: "and now I will
      show you the truth"   11:2a
    B. Regnal prophecy of a succession of kings,
      introduced by such phrases as "a king shall
      arise"   11:2b-45
      1. The Persian era ("three more kings shall
        arise")   2b
      2. Career of Alexander ("a mighty king
        shall arise")   3-4
      3. The rise of the Ptolemies, to the first
        interdynastic marriage   5-6
      4. War between Egypt and Syria   7-9
      5. Career of Antiochus III   10-19
        a. First campaign against Egypt   10-12
        b. Second campaign against Egypt   13-15
        c. Triumphant phase (he shall do
          according to his own will)   16-18a
        d. Fall   18b-19
      6. Brief career of Seleucus IV   20
      7. Career of Antiochus Epiphanes   21-45
        a. His rise   21-24
        b. First campaign against Egypt   25-28

The major divisions in this unit coincide in several cases with shifts in the metaphysical levels involved. First, the apparition of the angel in II leads to an explanation of the metaphysical backdrop of the historical action in III. Then the angelic discourse switches back to narrate history in terms of human actions. The eschatological section of the discourse is marked by a return to the metaphysical plane, when "Michael shall arise." The supplementary vision focuses on the exact duration of the persecution. The repetition of concluding instructions (12:4, 9, 13) enhances the sense of closure at the end of this chapter.

Within the angelic discourse there is evident parallelism between the careers of Antiochus III and Antiochus IV. The latter clearly escalates matters by magnifying himself even against God, thereby moving events to a crisis, which is resolved in the eschatological conclusion.

The unity of this section has been questioned at several points: Hasslberger (p. 135) rejects 10:1 because it is in the third person, 10:2 lacks a connecting *wĕ* ("and"), 1b is superfluous, and the *ṣābā'* ("conflict") mentioned as the subject of the vision is never mentioned again. It is true that this verse provides a summary introduction to the revelation and therefore has an editorial quality, but this does not necessarily require separate authorship. Apocalyptic literature seldom conforms to modern standards of consistency and economy. The dating formula is also in the third person in ch. 7.

Hasslberger also regards 10:20–11:1 as secondary because he finds them awkward and partially repetitive of 10:12-14. Here again he seems to be imposing stylistic ideals on the text. Minor terminological variations (e.g., *śar pāras* for *śar malkût pāras*) cannot be taken as signs of a different hand. Other scholars have rejected 11:1 as an attempt "to identify the unknown *angelus revelator* of this apocalypse with the angel Gabriel in ch. 9," and therefore an editorial insertion (Hartman and DiLella, 276-77). We may question, however, whether the identification is necessarily secondary, if both chapters come from the same circle or even from the same author.

More substantive questions arise about the coherence of the epilogue, 12:5-13, with the rest of the unit. This passage is formally distinct since it contains a new vision. It serves as a conclusion to the whole book as well as to chs. 10–12. Yet it is not marked off by a new dating formula, as the other units are. The "two others" of 12:5 presuppose the revealing angel of ch. 10. Dan 12:9-10 echoes 11:35 and 12:4. The statement in 12:9 that "the words are shut up and sealed" appears to presuppose some lapse of time after the command to "shut up the words, and seal the book" in 12:4, but there is no adequate reason to posit different authorship.

Within the epilogue, the conflicting numbers in 12:11 and 12 can only be explained as successive attempts to give precision to the "time, two times, and half a time" of 12:7. Verse 11 was presumably added after the lapse of the 1150 days mentioned in 8:14, and 12:12 after the lapse of the number in 12:11.

Genre

Daniel 10:1–12:4 is in itself a complete "HISTORICAL" APOCALYPSE in the form of an EPIPHANY with an ANGELIC DISCOURSE. The epiphany is influenced by Ezekiel 1 and 8–10 and is itself echoed in Rev 1:13-15. The parallels with Isaiah 6 claimed by Nicol are on a more general level and of doubtful significance.

The epiphany is integrated here into an elaborate apocalypse which begins with an account of the circumstances and the predisposition of the seer, proceeds with the dialogue and angelic discourse, and concludes with the address by the angel in 12:4. The apocalyptic character of the revelation is assured by the role of the angelic "princes" and the explicit account of resurrection. The vision (*mar'eh*) referred to in 10:1, in parallel with *dābār* ("word"), presumably refers to the entire revelation, which begins with the epiphany. In the form of revelation Daniel 10–12 then resembles Daniel 9 rather than the symbolic visions of chs. 7 and 8.

Prior to the apparition, Daniel is said to be mourning and fasting. No cause for his grief is given here. Presumably it is related to his mourning in ch. 9, but we should note that fasting is often part of the process of receiving a vision; cf. *2 Bar.* 21:1; 47:2; 4 Ezra 5:20; 6:35; 9:24. (See Niditch, also Reid.)

The angelic discourse largely consists of the *ex eventu* REGNAL PROPHECY, which has affinities with Babylonian works such as the Dynastic Prophecy (Lambert). The main point of analogy lies in the use of anonymous formulas such as "a king will arise." The portrayal of Antiochus Epiphanes rising up "above every God" is "a reuse of the old Canaanite myth of the rebellion in the heavens which finds its OT reflex in such passages as Isa 14:3-21 and Ezek 28:1-19" (Clifford, 25). This myth is also reflected in Daniel 8.

An alternative interpretation has been put forward by Lebram, who holds that the historical material in Daniel 11 is derived from an Egyptian source and that the portrayal of Antiochus is modeled on Egyptian traditions about Cambyses as the evil king par excellence. It is not apparent, however, that Daniel's historical sources were Egyptian; indeed, the preponderant interest is in the careers of two Syrian kings, Antiochus III and IV. The motif of scaling heaven appears in a rather different way in the Middle Persian legend of Kay Kâûs (allegedly a name for Cambyses; see Lewy) who is carried up on a throne by an eagle. This legend does not, however, provide as good a parallel to Daniel as the myth of Helal ben Shachar in Isaiah 14. That Cambyses died in Syria on his way back to Persia (Herodotus *Hist.* 3.64) is taken by Lebram as the basis for the prediction that Antiochus would die in the land of Israel (Dan 11:40-45), but here again the parallel is not exact. A better parallel is surely the prophecy in Ezekiel 39 that Gog, the quasi-mythical eschatological adversary, would fall on the mountains of Israel. Lebram's study is valuable in that it draws attention to an Egyptian tradition which is phenomenologically similar to the portrayal of Antiochus here, even though it is not the most immediate background of the Danielic passage. (Note esp. the allusions to a hated "king from Syria" in the Potter's Oracle, an Egyptian political oracle which is similar in some respects to the historical apocalypses, and also the use of this Egyptian tradition in the Jewish *Sib. Or.* 3:611-15.)

Biblical allusions play an important part here as in other chapters of Daniel. H. L. Ginsberg has shown that the heroes of the book, the *maśkîlîm* ("wise teachers"), are modeled on the Suffering Servant of Isaiah 53. The term *maśkîl* itself may be adapted from the opening verse of the Servant poem—*hinnēh yaśkîl 'abdî* ("behold, my servant shall prosper," Isa 52:13). When the *maśkîlîm* are said to make the *rabbîm* ("many") understand and especially when the *maśkîlîm* are also described as *maṣdîqê hārabbîm* (lit. "those who justify the many") in 12:3, there is a direct allusion to Isa 53:11 ("my servant shall justify the many"). The exaltation of the servant then is the model for the *maśkîlîm*, who will shine like the stars. The use of Isaiah here does not determine the genre of the passage, which is not developed as a midrash on the Servant Song, but it obviously contributes to the meaning of Daniel.

The resurrection scene in Dan 12:1-3 has been characterized as a DESCRIPTION OF A JUDGMENT SCENE by Nickelsburg, who identifies the following constitutive elements:

(1) The witnesses: Michael, the angel defender; the angelic opponent is presupposed.
(2) The book of life.
(3) The resurrection, by which the dead participate in the judgment.
(4) The consequences of the judgment: vindication and condemnation.

It must also be said that crucial elements of the judgment scene are lacking, most notably the presiding judge. It is not clear that Michael serves as a witness here. (Nickelsburg assumes a confrontation of angelic advocates as in Zechariah 3.)

When Michael is said to arise (12:1) the reference may be to his victory in the heavenly battle. The allusion to the book of life certainly presupposes a judgment scene, but that scene is not described. Instead, Dan 12:1-3 is simply an ESCHATOLOGICAL PROPHECY.

The epilogue is a REVELATORY DIALOGUE, including a very brief description of the EPIPHANY of the angelic figures.

Setting

This is the only segment of Daniel that is dated to the reign of Cyrus the Persian by its introduction. It is thereby indicated as the last segment of the book. The forward glance to the "prince of Greece" in 10:20 completes the four-kingdom sequence and adds to the impression of finality.

The actual historical setting is evident in ch. 11. As Porphyry already observed, the prophecy is correct down to the career of Antiochus Epiphanes but not in the prediction of his death. The conservative argument that the concluding verses refer to the Antichrist of a distant eschaton is gratuitous: the text gives no indication of a change of referent. The author knows Antiochus's two campaigns against Egypt, the desecration of the temple in Jerusalem, and the fortification of the Akra, but not the reconsecration of the temple or the actual death of the king in late 164 B.C. Daniel 10–12 must have been written in the intervening period, between late 167 and late 164 B.C. It is evident from 11:33-35 that it was written in the heat of the persecution (cf. 1 Macc 1:54-64; 2 Maccabees 6–7). There is no evidence of a significant time lapse between the composition of chs. 8, 9, and 10–12, and as we have seen Daniel 7 may be no more than a few months older than Daniel 8.

Daniel 11 also gives some indication of the circles in which the book was written. The heroes of the persecution are the *maśkîlîm* or wise teachers, and they are singled out for special honor in the resurrection. Their role is to make the *rabbîm*, or masses, understand and to turn them to righteousness. The understanding they convey is presumably that which is contained in the book of Daniel itself. Their death is construed as a substitute for cultic purification, but they are not said to be priests. Distress over the disruption of the temple cult is not necessarily a mark of priestly authorship. Daniel 11 makes no mention of the Maccabees. The "little help" in Dan 11:34 has often been taken, since Porphyry, as a reference to the Maccabees, but this is doubtful. There is no hint of militancy in Daniel and the author would scarcely have regarded the Maccabees as a help in the task of making the masses understand. The "little help" is more likely to refer to the few who shared the viewpoint of the *maśkîlîm*. Again, the popular identification with the Hasidim of the Maccabean books is ill founded, since these were "mighty warriors of Israel" (1 Macc 2:42) who supported Judas enthusiastically (2 Macc 14:6) until the arrival of Alcimus. All we are told about the *maśkîlîm* is that they were teachers. If they were scribes, they were quite different from the scribalism of Ben Sira, in view of their visionary inclination.

The author of Daniel puts the blame for the persecution squarely on Antiochus Epiphanes, but he is said to give heed to those who forsake the holy covenant (11:30). This must surely be read as an allusion to the so-called Hellenistic Reform described in 1 and 2 Maccabees (pace Lebram, "Apokalyptik"). Daniel's perspective, however, is that of the world-kingdoms rather than of the internal Jewish tensions. The career of Epiphanes is viewed in the context of Hellenistic history, and is anticipated, in a lesser degree, by the career of Antiochus III. It cannot be said that Daniel takes sides in the struggles between the Seleucids and the Ptolemies. He is vehemently anti-Seleucid but at no point is there any hint of pro-Ptolemaic sympathies, and the Ptolemies do not figure in the predictions about the time of the end. (Contrast the pro-Ptolemaic Jewish *Sibylline Oracles* 3 in this regard.)

The specific dates in 12:11-12 are later additions which extend slightly the three and a half years of 12:7. What is remarkable is that these additions must have been made *after* the rededication of the temple, which took place three years after its desecration (1 Macc 4:54). This fact has some implications for the intention of the book.

Intention

The intention of Daniel 10–12 is evidently to console and exhort the persecuted Jews, but this formulation does not do full justice to the rhetorical effect of the apocalypse.

First, we are alerted in 10:1 that the effect of the revelation is *understanding*, and in 10:14 the angel says explicitly that he "came to make you *understand* what is to befall your people in the latter days." The understanding conveyed by the angel has its counterpart in the understanding which the *maśkîlîm* impart to the *rabbîm*. It consists not only of the historical prophecy but also of its metaphysical backdrop. The conflict of Michael and Gabriel with the heavenly "princes" of Persia and Greece is even more important than the earthly battles. The resolution of history comes in 12:1 when Michael arises, not when Judas Maccabee or any other human leader is victorious. Since this angelic activity is not immediately obvious in history it is especially crucial to the revealed understanding.

Second, the use of *ex eventu* prophecy is significant. It integrates the focal events of the Maccabean era into the sequence of history and permits the clarification of Epiphanes' career by showing a similar tendency earlier in the dynasty. More fundamentally, it builds the assurance that all is predetermined, since so much can be "predicted" accurately. The *ex eventu* prophecy, then, augments the epiphany as a means of lending authority to the real prophecies of the death of the king and the resurrection.

Third, the group which is comforted is specified more narrowly in view of the division within the Jewish community that is evident in 11:30-35. There is a sharp distinction between those who violate the covenant and those who know their God. The community which will be saved does not include the whole Jewish people, and the *maśkîlîm* stand out as a special class within it.

Finally, the specific hope which is offered is important. It involves not only the death of the persecutor and the victory of the angel Michael, but also the resurrection of the dead. This hope responds directly to the dilemma of the persecution. It does not propose a general resurrection, but "many" will rise, some to everlasting life, some to everlasting contempt. Again, the *maśkîlîm* are singled out. They will "shine like the stars," which in apocalyptic idiom means to become companions to the angelic host (cf. *1 Enoch* 104:2, 4, 6). The *maśkîlîm*, then, can afford to lose their lives in this world since they are assured of glory in the next. The prophecy of resurrection is not "temporally indeterminate" (Hasslberger,

316). The expression "at that time" indicates direct continuity with the events of ch. 11.

The hope of resurrection is mentioned in Daniel only in the concluding chapter. Daniel 7 had spoken of a kingdom, and Daniel 8 and 9 seemed primarily concerned with the restoration of the temple. The question arises how these hopes are related to each other. There are two possible ways of approaching this question. One would suppose a chronological development in the different chapters. The other would view them as complementary panels which together make up a multifaceted whole.

The argument for chronological development is a precarious one. All four units in Daniel 7–12 were composed within a very short time. Even if Daniel 7 is ascribed to a different author, by reason of style and language, it is clear that the author of Daniel 8 followed him closely and must have belonged to the same circle. All four units contain a review of history prior to Antiochus Epiphanes, focus on the career of Epiphanes, and predict his demise by supernatural power. All four see Epiphanes' rebellion against God as the heart of the matter. (Daniel 9 is least clear in this regard: it speaks of Epiphanes as "the prince who is to come" and "the desolator.") The desecration of the temple is most prominent in chs. 8 and 9 but it also figures in ch. 11, and ch. 7 notes that Epiphanes "shall think to change the times and the law," a reference to the disruption of the cultic calendar. Even in the expectations of salvation there is no necessary contradiction. Daniel 7 does not address the fate of individuals and Daniel 12 does not address the public aspects of salvation. Neither chapter claims to give an exclusive or complete picture. In fact, the "kingdom" of ch. 7 is notoriously vague. It appears to have two dimensions, the dominion of the angelic holy ones and the kingdom of the Jewish "people of the holy ones" on earth. Since the kingdom is awarded in a heavenly judgment scene, its relation to the historical, political order is less than clear. Moreover, Daniel 11–12 never says that all history will cease. The selective resurrection of the dead is not incompatible with an ongoing Jewish kingdom. It should, of course, be clear that a new era is involved, one which is drastically different from all that has gone before. The state of salvation cannot simply be equated with the restoration of the temple or the end of the persecution (pace Hasslberger, 316). Even in ch. 9 the "end" also involves the end of transgression and the beginning of everlasting righteousness.

The visions were surely understood as complementary by the person who put the book together, and there is no good evidence that this person was anyone other than the author of chs. 8–12. Even if the belief in resurrection came to the author at a relatively late stage in the composition of the book, all the eschatological visions must now be read in the light of it. In fact, there is no compelling evidence that ch. 12 represents a change in the theology of the visions.

The placing of the prophecy of resurrection at the end of the book can be explained more satisfactorily by the stylistic reason that it is a climactic revelation. Daniel 10–12 is by far the longest unit in the book. It is also by far the most detailed in its discussion of the historical context and the clearest in its presentation of the metaphysical backdrop. This long revelation builds up to the announcement of resurrection, which is the last substantive revelation of the book. It is also the most distinctive revelation of Daniel, over against earlier prophetic and, more generally, biblical tradition (Collins, "Eschatology"; the belief may be attested earlier in some of the *Enoch* writings). There is no doubt that Daniel 10–12 clarifies the historical context of all the visions and it may be taken to clarify the mythological and eschatological dimensions in a similar way. The "kingdom" of ch. 7 is then seen in a new light. What is at issue is not just a new political administration or even the restoration of the temple, but a new order where the faithful community shares the power of the heavenly holy ones and the wise teachers shine with them in eternal life.

The brief epilogue focuses again on the question of time, which has also played a part in the earlier visions. The attempt to specify the time makes the assurance of the prediction more concrete and therefore more comforting. The initial figure, a time, two times, and half a time, in 12:7 was already given in ch. 7. The glosses in 12:11 and 12, however, must be seen as revisions of the figure in 8:14. Here we are presumably dealing with a case of "cognitive dissonance" (Festinger, Carroll). When the prophecy had not been fulfilled by the specified time, the figures were revised. These revisions must have taken place after the rededication of the temple by Judas Maccabee. Yet the redactor, at least (he may also have been the author), did not regard the prophecy as fulfilled. The promise of the angel in 12:7 was that "all these things would be accomplished"; i.e., transgression would cease, an era of righteousness would begin, the dead would be resurrected, and the "people of the holy ones" would receive dominion over all the kingdoms under heaven. Obviously, none of this had happened. Remarkably, the contradictory numbers were allowed to remain side by side. The exact date was not ultimately so important, or perhaps it was regarded as yet another of the mysteries that was only revealed in a symbolic code.

Bibliography

R. P. Carroll, *When Prophecy Failed: Cognitive Dissonance in the Prophetic Traditions of the Old Testament* (New York: Seabury, 1979); R. J. Clifford, "History and Myth in Daniel 10–12," *BASOR* 220 (1975) 23-26; J. J. Collins, "Apocalyptic Eschatology as the Transcendence of Death," in *Visionaries and Their Apocalypses* (ed. P. D. Hanson; Philadelphia: Fortress, 1983) 61-84 (repr. from *CBQ* 36 [1974] 21-43); L. Festinger, *A Theory of Cognitive Dissonance* (Evanston: Row, Peterson & Co., 1957); H. L. Ginsberg, "The Oldest Interpretation of the Suffering Servant," *VT* 3 (1953) 400-404; B. Hasslberger, *Hoffnung in der Bedrängnis* (St. Ottilien: Eos Verlag, 1977) 111-374; W. G. Lambert, *The Background of Jewish Apocalyptic* (London: Athlone Press, 1978); J. C. H. Lebram, "Apokalyptik und Hellenismus im Buch Daniel," *VT* 20 (1970) 503-24; idem, "König Antiochus im Buch Daniel," *VT* 25 (1975) 737-72; H. Lewy, "The Babylonian Background of the Kay Kâûs Legend," *ArOr* XVII, 2 (1949) 28-109; B. Nicol, "Isaiah's Vision and the Visions of Daniel," *VT* 29 (1979) 501-4; G. W. Nickelsburg, *Resurrection, Immortality, and Eternal Life in Intertestamental Judaism* (HTS 26; Cambridge, Mass.: Harvard University Press, 1972) 11-27; S. Niditch, "The Visionary," in *Ideal Figures in Ancient Judaism* (ed. J. J. Collins and G. W. Nickelsburg; Chico: Scholars Press, 1980) 153-79; S. B. Reid, "The Sociological Setting of the Historical Apocalypses of I Enoch and the Book of Daniel" (Diss., Emory University, 1981).

GLOSSARY

ACCUSATION (Anklage). A speech alleging that someone has broken the law or otherwise done wrong. This speech form had its original setting in judicial practice, but was adapted by the prophets and could be used in a literary context. It may be addressed directly to the accused or refer to them in the third person. The simplest form of an accusation is a declaratory sentence (cf. 2 Sam 12:9b; Jer 29:21, 23) or accusing question (2 Sam 12:9a; Jer 22:15). A more developed form establishes a causal connection between the offense and its consequence (cf. 1 Sam 15:23).

Related genres: (→) Indictment Speech, (→) Admonition, (→) Covenant Lawsuit.

C. Westermann, *Basic Forms of Prophetic Speech* (tr. H. C. White; Philadelphia: Westminster, 1967) 142-48.

ADMONITION (Mahnung, Mahnrede). An address designed to dissuade an individual or a group from a certain type of conduct. It is widely attested in the prophetic and wisdom literature and occasionally in apocalyptic books (e.g., Dan 4:24 [*RSV* 27]).

ANGELIC DISCOURSE (Rede eines Engels, Gespräch zwischen Engeln). A revelation delivered as a speech by an angel, often as a constituent of an (→) apocalypse or vision. It may follow an (→) epiphany as in Daniel 10–11 or be reported without visual element as in *Jub.* 2:1ff. The most plausible background is in the message dreams of the ancient Near East.

Related genre: (→) Apocalypse.

APOCALYPSE (Apokalypse). A genre of revelatory literature with a narrative framework, in which a revelation is mediated by an otherworldly being to a human recipient, disclosing a transcendent reality which is both temporal, in that it envisages eschatological salvation, and spatial, in that it involves another, supernatural, world.

The two main subgenres are apocalypses with or without an otherworldly journey. The point at issue here is not the presence or absence of a single motif, since the otherworldly journey provides the context for the revelation and determines the form of the work (cf. *1 Enoch* 1–36; *2 Enoch*; *3 Baruch*). All the Jewish apocalypses which are not otherworldly journeys have a review of history in some form and may be conveniently labeled "historical" apocalypses (cf. Daniel; the *Animal Apocalypse* and *Apocalypse of Weeks* in *1 Enoch*; *4 Ezra*; *2 Baruch*).

The genre functions to provide a view of the world that will be a source of consolation in the face of distress and a support and authorization for whatever course of action is recommended, and to invest this worldview with the status of supernatural revelation.

The genre is attested in Persian and Greco-Roman literature as well as in the Jewish and Christian corpora. Apocalypses generally presuppose a crisis of some kind, but the specific kind of crisis may vary widely.

Related genres: (→) Oracle, (→) Testament, (→) Symbolic Vision.

J. J. Collins, ed., *Semeia 14: Apocalypse: The Morphology of a Genre* (Missoula: Scholars Press, 1979); idem, *The Apocalyptic Imagination in Ancient Judaism* (New York: Crossroad, 1984); P. Hanson, "Apocalypse, Genre," *IDBSup*; L. Hartman, "Survey of the Problem of Apocalyptic Genre," in *Apocalypticism in the Mediterranean World and the Near East* (ed. D. Hellholm; Tübingen: Mohr, 1983) 329-43; D. Hellholm, "The Problem of Apocalyptic Genre and the Apocalypse of John," SBLASP 21 (1982) 157-98.

ARETALOGICAL NARRATIVE (aretalogische-romanhafte Erzählung). The aretalogical narrative is a wonderful and miraculous story which redounds to the glory of a god. It has been proposed as a characterization of Jonah, Judith, the story of Heliodorus in 2 Maccabees 3, and Daniel 2–6 (Hengel). It overlaps to a considerable degree with (→) legend, since both are concerned with the wonderful and miraculous. The appropriateness of the designation for Jonah and Judith may be questioned.

Related genre: (→) Legend.

M. Hengel, *Judaism and Hellenism* (tr. J. Bowden; Philadelphia: Fortress, 1974) 1.110-12.

COMMUNAL CONFESSION OF SIN (Sündenbekenntnis des Volkes, gemeinsames Sündenbekenntnis). Prayer of repentance and petition for mercy, closely related to the so-called (→) covenant form. Typically it involves a confession of breach of covenant, an admission of God's righteousness, a recollection of God's mercy, and an appeal for mercy for God's own sake. Cf. Dan 9:4b-19; Psalm 106; Ezra 9:6-15; Neh 1:5-11; 9:5-37; Bar 1:15–3:8; and the "Words of the Luminaries" from Qumran.

H. Gunkel and J. Begrich, *Einleitung in die Psalmen* (HKAT 1/1; Göttingen: Vandenhoeck & Ruprecht, 1933) 117-39; O. H. Steck, *Israel und das gewaltsame Geschick der Propheten* (Neukirchen-Vluyn: Neukirchener, 1967) 110-36; C. Westermann, "Struktur und Geschichte der Klage im Alten Testament," *ZAW* 66 (1954) 44-80.

COURT LEGEND (Hoflegende). A (→) legend set in a royal court, or a (→) court tale concerned with the wonderful and aimed at edification. (Cf. Daniel 1–6.)

COURT TALE (Hofgeschichte). A story set in a royal court. Cf. the Joseph story, Esther, Daniel 1–6, and the nonbiblical tale of Aḥiqar. This categorization is based on setting rather than form or content and is compatible with various genres, e.g., (→) novella or (→) legend. Ancient Near Eastern court tales do, however, have stereotypical plots, e.g., the subcategories (→) tale of court contest and (→) tale of court conflict.

W. L. Humphreys, "A Life-Style for Diaspora: A Study of the Tales of Esther and Daniel," *JBL* 92 (1973) 211-23; D. B. Redford, *A Study of the Biblical Story of Joseph* (VTSup 20; Leiden: Brill, 1970).

COVENANT FORM (Bundesformular). A reconstruction of the structure of the Mosaic covenant based on analogies with Hittite suzerainty treaties. A typical treaty has six parts: (1) the preamble; (2) the historical prologue; (3) the stipulations; (4) provisions for deposit of the text and for public reading; (5) list of divine witnesses; and (6) blessings and curses. No biblical text reproduces all of these elements, although significant clusters of them are present in some covenantal passages (Exodus 20; Joshua 24; and esp. the book of Deuteronomy). There are also analogies with Assyrian treaties from the first millennium, so the comparison with the older Hittite treaties does not necessarily establish a premonarchical date for the covenant. The core of this "covenant form" lies in the idea that the stipulations derive their force from two sources: the recollection of history and the prospect of curses or blessings. This core structure plays a prominent part in the prophetic books (possibly under Deuteronomic influence; cf. Amos 2:6-16) and in a series of postexilic prayers which are primarily (→) communal confessions of sin (cf. Dan 9:4b-19; Ezra 9:6-15; Neh 9:5-37; Bar 1:15–3:8). The original setting of the form was in the world of international relations. Some scholars believe that it was given a liturgical setting in a covenant renewal ceremony, but this remains hypothetical.

Related genres: (→) Covenant Lawsuit, (→) Communal Confession of Sin.

K. Baltzer, *The Covenant Formulary* (tr. D. Green; Philadelphia: Fortress, 1971); D. J. McCarthy, *Treaty and Covenant* (rev. ed.; AnBib 21A; Rome: Pontifical Biblical Institute, 1978); G. E. Mendenhall, *Law and Covenant in Israel and the Ancient Near East* (Pittsburgh: Biblical Colloquium, 1955).

COVENANT LAWSUIT (Rechtsstreit, Prozess bezüglich des Bundes). A form of (→) indictment speech against the people of Israel, spoken by a prophet in the name of God. The people is convicted of breaking the covenant law. The indictment is grounded in the recollection of God's acts of deliverance, which created the obligation of loyalty, and the curses which are incurred are either stated or implied. The use of this form may be due to Deuteronomic influence, but this is disputed. Cf. Amos 2:6-16; Mic 6:1-8; Jer 2:4-13; Deuteronomy 32. The appropriateness of the term "lawsuit" has been challenged since there is no appeal to a third party as arbitrator.

Related genres: (→) Covenant Form, (→) Indictment Speech, (→) Judgment Speech, (→) Accusation.

J. Harvey, *Le plaidoyer prophétique contre Israël après la rupture de l'alliance* (Bruges: Desclée de Brouwer, 1967); H. B. Huffmon, "The Covenant Lawsuit in the Prophets," *JBL* 78 (1959) 285-95; K. Nielsen, *Yahweh as Prosecutor and Judge: An Investigation of the Prophetic Lawsuit (Rîb-Pattern)* (tr. F. Cryer; JSOTSup 9; Sheffield: University of Sheffield, 1978); M. de Roche, "Yahweh's *rîb* Against Israel: A Reassessment of the So-Called 'Prophetic Lawsuit' in the Preexilic Prophets," *JBL* 102 (1983) 563-74; G. E. Wright, "The Lawsuit of God," in *Israel's Prophetic Heritage*

(Fest. J. Muilenburg; ed. B. W. Anderson and W. Harrelson; New York: Harper & Row, 1962) 26-67.

DECREE (Dekret). A proclamation issued or authorized by a king or other person in authority, containing prescriptions which have the force of law. Cf. Dan 3:31 *(RSV* 4:1); Ezra 6:3-12; 7:12-26; Esth 8:9-14. Decrees are often promulgated in epistolary form.

Related genre: (→) Proclamation.

DESCRIPTION OF JUDGMENT SCENE (Beschreibung einer Gerichtsszene). The basic features of these scenes are the enthronement of a heavenly judge and the execution of the judgment. Other common motifs include the opening of the books, an address to the condemned, and their recognition of their situation. Judgment scenes may focus on the judgment of nations (cf. Daniel 7; *1 Enoch* 90:20-38) or of individuals (e.g., *Testament of Abraham*). They are found frequently, but not exclusively, in apocalypses. They serve to clarify the ultimate values in life.

G. W. Nickelsburg, "Eschatology in the Testament of Abraham: A Study of the Judgment Scene in the Two Recensions," in *Studies on the Testament of Abraham* (ed. G. W. Nickelsburg; Missoula: Scholars Press, 1976) 23-64.

DIASPORA NOVELLA (Diasporanovelle). A (→) novella set in the Jewish Diaspora. Cf. Esther. This categorization is based on the setting of certain Jewish tales but neglects their affinities with other Near Eastern tales and with folklore in general.

A. Meinhold, "Die Gattung der Josephsgeschichte und des Estherbuches: Diasporanovelle, I, II," *ZAW* 87 (1975) 306-24; 88 (1976) 79-93.

DOXOLOGY (Doxologie). A short (→) hymn of praise which declares God (or God's name) blessed and then states a reason. The genre had its setting in the temple cult (cf. Psalms 96–98, 117, 145–150) but also acquired a literary usage (cf. Dan 2:20-23; 3:28, 33 [*RSV* 4:3]; 4:31-32 [*RSV* 34-35]).

Related genre: (→) Hymn of Praise.

E. Gerstenberger, "Psalms," in *Old Testament Form Criticism* (ed. J. H. Hayes; TUMSR 2; San Antonio: Trinity University Press, 1974) 208-9; C. Westermann, *The Praise of God in the Psalms* (tr. K. Crim; Richmond: John Knox, 1965) 122-32.

DREAM INTERPRETATION (Traumdeutung). A speech structured in response to a (→) dream report, following the major structural elements of the dream report.

The interpretation process reflects the work of a professional dream interpreter. The interpretation can, however, develop its lines of structure on the basis of allegory, and thus show a certain amount of freedom from the explicit lines of the (→) dream report (cf. Gen 41:25-32).

DREAM REPORT (Traumbericht), DREAM VISION (Traumschilderung). A report in the first or third person designed to recount the principal elements of a dream experience. Typical dream reports of the ancient Near East appear within a conventional frame. This consists of an introduction, which tells about the dreamer, locality, and other circumstances, and a conclusion, which describes the end of the dream and often includes the reaction of the dreamer or the fulfillment of the dream. The actual report of the dream makes extensive use of verbs meaning "dream" and particles meaning "behold." Cf. Gen 37:5-11; 40:9-11, 16-17; 41:1-8; Dan 2:25-45; 4:1-30 (*RSV* 4-33).

Related genre: (→) Symbolic Dream Vision.

E. L. Ehrlich, *Der Traum im alten Testament* (BZAW 73; Berlin: Töpelmann, 1953); A. L. Oppenheim, *The Interpretation of Dreams in the Ancient Near East* (Philadelphia: American Philosophical Society, 1956); W. Richter, "Traum und Traumdeutung im AT: Ihre Form und Verwendung," *BZ* 7 (1963) 202-20.

EPIPHANY (Epiphanie). A vision of a single supernatural figure. This figure may then function as a revealer (cf. Ezekiel 8; Daniel 10). An epiphany can also take place within the context of a larger vision (cf. the "one like a son of man" in Daniel 7 or the "man from the sea" in 4 Ezra 13).

Related genres: (→) Apocalypse, (→) Theophany.

Jörg Jeremias, *Theophanie: Die Geschichte einer alttestamentlichen Gattung* (WMANT 10; Neukirchen-Vluyn: Neukirchener, 1965).

EPISTLE (Brief, Epistel). A subgenre of (→) letter that is an artistic literary form and is public in character, e.g., letters conveying royal decrees (Ezra 7:12-26) and proclamations (Dan 3:31–4:34 [*RSV* 4:1-37]). A clear distinction between epistles and other letters cannot always be maintained (e.g., in the case of Paul).

Related genre: (→) Letter.

A. Deissmann, *Light from the Ancient East* (tr. L. R. M. Strachan; 4th ed.; 1927; repr. Grand Rapids: Baker, 1978); J. L. White, ed., *Semeia 22: Studies in Ancient Letter Writing* (Chico: Scholars Press, 1982).

ESCHATOLOGICAL PROPHECY/PREDICTION (eschatologische Prophezeiung). Prophecy relating to the end time, when the conditions of this world will be radically changed. Cf. Isa 11:1-9; 65:17-25; Dan 12:1-3.

Related form: (→) Prophecy of Cosmic Transformation.

EX EVENTU PROPHECY (Prophezeiung ex eventu). Presentation of events which have already taken place in the guise of future prophecy. This device is a constituent of several genres (→ oracle, → testament, → apocalypse) and is found already in Genesis (e.g., Gen 15:17-21). An elaborate example is found in Daniel 11.

FULFILLMENT FORMULA (Erfüllungsformel). Statement that a prediction has been fulfilled. Cf. Dan 4:25-30 (*RSV* 28-33).

FÜRSTENSPIEGEL. Admonitions addressed to a king (cf. Dan 4:24 [*RSV* 27]). The so-called Babylonian *Fürstenspiegel* has a distinctive form since it follows the style of omen interpretation with a protasis and apodosis. This Babylonian form is not used in the OT.

Related genre: (→) Admonition.

W. G. Lambert, *Babylonian Wisdom Literature* (Oxford: Clarendon, 1960) 112-15.

"HISTORICAL" APOCALYPSE (Apokalypse bezüglich der Geschichte). A subgenre of apocalypse characterized by the lack of an (→) otherworldly journey and the inclusion of an (→) *ex eventu* prophecy of history. The most typical form of revelation is (→) the symbolic dream vision. The content typically includes an *ex eventu* prediction of the course of history, often divided into a set number of periods (→ periodization), followed by eschatological woes and upheavals which are (→) signs of the end, judgment, and salvation. Apocalyptic eschatology, even in the "historical" apocalypses, typically involves the resurrection of the dead. The "historical" apocalypses are usually related to an historical crisis, e.g., the persecution of the Maccabean era or the fall of Jerusalem. Cf. Daniel 7–12; *1 Enoch* 83–90; 4 Ezra; *2 Baruch.*

Related genres: (→) Apocalypse, (→) Oracle, (→) Testament.

J. J. Collins, "The Jewish Apocalypses," in *Semeia 14: Apocalypse: The Morphology of a Genre* (ed. J. J. Collins; Missoula: Scholars Press, 1979) 30-36.

HISTORY (Geschichtsschreibung). A written narrative of past events that is governed by facts, as far as the writer could ascertain and interpret them, and not by traditional or aesthetic principles of organization. History therefore does not structure its narrative according to a plot acceptable because of its familiarity (as in a traditional epic) or because of its intrigue or construction (as in romance or novel). Rather, history seeks an objective structure, based on chronological or causal sequence, such that, ideally, another historian dealing with the same events would reproduce the same structure.

However, the difference between history, with its allegiance to fact as its ordering principle, and fictional (→) narrative, with its traditional or aesthetic ordering, is not absolute. Both the structures used by the two kinds of narration and the problems associated with the concept "fact" affect the distinction between the two. As far as structures are concerned, fiction incorporates logical features proper to history (human causality, chronology) and history reflects elements from the fictional. This latter fact is evident in ancient times: The "Succession Narrative" (2 Samuel 9–20; 1 Kings 1–2) reflects the "royal novel" of Egypt, Herodotus (the Homeric Epic), and Thucydides' Attic tragedy. In modern times, history writing has often been influenced by the technique of the novel.

Then there is the concept "fact." Historical events, "facts," are accessible only through evidence. There are no "brute facts"; interpretation is to some extent inherent to all "facts." This is particularly true of history, where the evidence is often difficult to find and to interpret. This means that in all historical narrative, the facts are selected and the pattern in which they are presented is arranged according to the writer's ability to find evidence and to judge it. The narrative is dependent upon the criteria which the writer thought relevant to a critical judgment about the reality of alleged facts, and on the views which guided his judgment about what was important, either as event or as explanation of event. Hence all history is selective and interpretative. It remains formal history if allegiance to fact (as far as possible) is its fundamental structural principle.

R. G. Collingwood, *The Idea of History* (Oxford: Oxford University Press, 1946); Van A. Harvey, *The Historian and the Believer* (New York: Macmillan, 1966); H. White, *Metahistory* (Baltimore: Johns Hopkins University Press, 1973); J. Van Seters, *In Search of History: Historiography in the Ancient World and the Origins of Biblical History* (New Haven: Yale University Press, 1983).

HYMN OF PRAISE (Loblied). General designation for any formal poetic praise of God. Westermann distinguishes between declarative psalms of praise (thanksgiving hymns) and descriptive praise. All the descriptive psalms of praise begin with an imperative call to praise. In most, the reason for praise follows (cf. Psalm 117). Westermann further distinguishes a group of "imperative psalms," which are characterized by their increased use of imperatives (cf. Psalms 100, 145, 148, 150, and the "Song of the Three Young Men" in the Additions to Daniel).

Related genre: (→) Doxology.

C. Westermann, *The Praise of God in the Psalms* (tr. K. Crim; Richmond: John Knox, 1965) 116-51.

INDICTMENT SPEECH (Anklagerede). A speech which both formulates an (→) accusation and declares the sentence. It is typical of prophetic judgment speeches (cf. Amos 2:6-16). The original setting was in juridical practice but it was also adapted to purely literary contexts (e.g., Dan 5:17-28).

C. Westermann, *Basic Forms of Prophetic Speech* (tr. H. C. White; Philadelphia: Westminster, 1967) 129-209.

INTERROGATION (Vernehmung, Verhör). Examination of a person on trial by the presiding judge (cf. Dan 3:13-18). It is a common element in martyr stories (cf. 2 Maccabees 7). The original setting was presumably in judicial procedure.

LEGEND (Legende). A (→) narrative primarily concerned with the wonderful and aimed at edification (cf. the stories in Daniel 1–6).

The legend has no specific structure of its own. It is concerned not with narrative interest, but with the impressiveness of its contents, which are supposed to stimulate its audience to believe or to do something good. Thus legends often serve to inculcate awe for holy places (cf. Judg 6:11-24) and for ritual practices (cf. 2 Macc 1:19-22), and respect for individuals (cf. the Elijah Cycle; 2 Kgs 2:23-24) who may be models of devotion and virtue (cf. Exod 32:27-29; Deut 33:9; Num 25:6-12; Ps 106:30-31). This function parallels the usage in the ancient world where legends were told to glorify shrines, the ritual practices observed in them, and the heroes whose connection with the place honored it (cf. Herodotus *Hist.* 2 for Egypt; Pausanius *Description of Greece*).

Legend is distinguished from (→) *Märchen,* a genre which shares an interest in the wonderful, by virtue of two characteristics: (1) its specific practical aim (*Märchen* may have a moral, but it is concerned more with general attitudes), and (2) its claim to belief. Unlike the *Märchen,* the legend is placed in the real world and is often associated with historical characters. This latter characteristic distinguishes legend from (→) myth, which may claim belief but is essentially nonhistorical, outside time. Legend is distinguished from (→) story by (1) its specific practical aim, and (2) its consequent relative indifference to narrative art. It is the marvelous and not the story line that constitutes the legend's essential claim on attention.

H. Delehaye, *The Legends of the Saints* (tr. V. M. Crawford; London:

Longmans, Green, 1962); R. Hals, "Legend: A Case Study in OT Form-Critical Terminology," *CBQ* 34 (1972) 166-76; H. Rosenfeld, *Legende* (Sammlung Metzler 9; Stuttgart: J. B. Metzler, 1972) 5-6, 15-17; S. Thompson, *The Folktale* (New York: Dryden Press, 1946) 234-71.

LETTER (Brief). A written communication from one person or group to another. Semitic letters usually consist of an epistolary prescript and the body of the letter. Postscripts and closing formulas are rare in Mesopotamian letters and do not occur in the OT. By contrast, a formulaic word of farewell is found in a majority of Greek letters. Farewell formulas are found in the Hebrew and Aramaic Bar Kokhba letters.

The prescript identifies the sender and the addressee and usually includes an initial greeting, often joined directly to the address. In Semitic letters, the greeting is usually more than a single word. In Greek letters the greeting is often a single word, but a brief wish of good health may sometimes be added. The one-word greeting is found in the Hebrew Bar Kokhba letters and in rabbinic letters. In Hebrew and Aramaic letters the body is often introduced by the expression "and now" (cf. 2 Kgs 10:2).

Some scholars distinguish between a letter as "a means of communication between persons who are separated from each other" and an (→) epistle as "an artistic literary form," which is public rather than private. The distinction is difficult to maintain in some cases but does indicate two poles of a continuum. All the letters in the OT are official or formal in character; personal or private correspondence is not attested.

Different types of letters can be distinguished by content, situation, or intention. Biblical letters include written orders and instructions (cf. Ezra 4:17-22), royal decrees (Ezra 7:12-26), reports (Ezra 4:11-16; 5:7b-17), or even a prophetic speech (Jeremiah 29).

Related genre: (→) Epistle.

A. Deissmann, *Light from the Ancient East* (tr. L. R. M. Strachan; 4th ed.; 1927; repr. Grand Rapids: Baker, 1978); D. Pardee, et al., "An Overview of Ancient Hebrew Epistolography," *JBL* 97 (1978) 321-46; idem, *Handbook of Ancient Hebrew Letters* (Chico: Scholars Press, 1982); J. L. White, ed., *Semeia 22: Studies in Ancient Letter Writing* (Chico: Scholars Press, 1982).

LIST (Liste). A simple enumeration of names or items.

LISTS OF REVEALED THINGS (Listen geoffenbarter Dinge). Summary lists of revealed secrets are found in a number of (→) apocalypses: *1 Enoch* 41:1-7; 43:1-2; 60:11-22; *2 Enoch* 23:1; 40:1-13; *2 Bar.* 59:5-11. They are primarily concerned with cosmological secrets but also include matters of eschatological interest such as the abodes of the dead. These lists have been related to the wisdom tradition as exemplified by Job 38.

M. E. Stone, "Lists of Revealed Things in the Apocalyptic Literature," in *Magnalia Dei: The Mighty Acts of God* (*Fest.* G. E. Wright; ed. F. M. Cross, W. E. Lemke, and P. D. Miller; Garden City: Doubleday, 1976) 414-52.

LISTS OF VICES AND VIRTUES (Tugend- und Lasterkataloge). Catalogs of sins and virtuous acts are found in several literary genres in the Hellenistic age. They are characteristic of Greek popular philosophy and were taken over by Paul and Philo. They are also found in (→) apocalypses, (→) oracles, and (→) testaments. Their setting was in moral instruction and popular preaching.

H. Conzelmann, *1 Corinthians* (tr. J. W. Leitch; Hermeneia; Philadelphia: Fortress, 1975) 100-101; A. Vögtle, *Die Tugend- und Lasterkataloge im Neuen Testament* (NTAbh 16/4.5 Münster: Aschendorff, 1936).

MÄRCHEN. A traditional narrative set in a mysterious world of fantasy, provoking sympathy for the principal figure. It commonly features creatures such as goblins, demons, sprites, and talking animals. A recurring motif is a concern to show how a basic injustice was finally righted. Cf. Num 22:21-35.

Related genres: (→) Narrative, (→) Tale.

A. Jolles, *Einfache Formen* (2nd ed.; Tübingen: Niemeyer, 1958).

MARTYR LEGEND (Märtyrerlegende). A (→) legend which recounts the trial, sufferings, and death of a person who is persecuted for religious reasons. (Cf. 2 Maccabees 7.)

Related genre: (→) Legend.

H. A. Fischel, "Martyr and Prophet," *JQR* 37 (1946-47) 265-80, 363-86; U. Kellermann, *Auferstanden in den Himmel: 2 Makkabäer 7 und die Auferstehung der Märtyrer* (Stuttgart: Katholisches Bibelwerk, 1979).

MIDRASH (Midrasch). "A work that attempts to make a text of Scripture understandable, useful and relevant for a later generation. It is the text of Scripture which is the point of departure and it is for the sake of the text that the midrash exists" (Wright, 74). Different kinds of midrash can be distinguished: homiletic, exegetical, or narrative. The primary corpus is found in the rabbinic literature.

The mere use of allusions to earlier biblical texts does not constitute a midrash, although the word is often used loosely in this sense. An exegetical midrash on Jer 25:11-12; 29:10 can be found in Daniel 9. Wisdom of Solomon 11–19 may be regarded as a homiletic midrash on Exod 12:37–17:7.

Related genre: (→) Pesher.

G. Porton, "Midrash: Palestinian Jews and the Hebrew Bible in the Greco-Roman Period," *ANRW* II.19.1 (1979) 103-38; A. G. Wright, *The Literary Genre Midrash* (Staten Island: Alba House, 1967).

MYTH (Mythos, Mythe). One can describe at least five major uses of the term myth:

(1) Any (→) narrative about gods or culture heroes. This is the terminology of the first form-critical work (cf. H. Gunkel, *Genesis* [HKAT I/1; Göttingen: Vandenhoeck & Ruprecht, 1964]).

(2) A narrative recited to accompany a ritual. Undoubtedly myth is so used in many cultures. However, the idea, once widely held, that all myth was created to account for or accompany ritual actions (Raglan, Hyman) is untenable. Myths have many different origins and functions (Kirk).

(3) A symbolic expression of certain basic intuitions in which intellectual and emotional perceptions are interfused. This is the reason for the recurrence of the same symbols in diverse cultures and in separate individual psychic experiences, as in dreams (Cassirer, Jung).

(4) A narrative which functions in the traditions of various cultures or in individual lives to constitute world order by referring important ele-

ments of experience effectively to a higher supernatural reality of primordial events (in *illo tempore,* Eliade).

(5) The narrative resolution of contradictory perceptions or experiences (Levi-Strauss).

Uses 3-5 may be more generally characterized as attempts to deal with the ultimate in terms of symbols structured in a narrative, rather than of a logical system. These uses refer to a mode of writing on a higher level of abstraction than genres such as (→) apocalypse or (→) prophecy; e.g., Isa 11:1-9 or Daniel 7 can be characterized as myth in this sense. In biblical studies the term myth is often used for allusions to polytheistic stories (cf. Psalm 82; Daniel 7), i.e., in use (1) above, and this usage may coincide with the characterization of a mode of writing (cf. Daniel 7).

E. Cassirer, *Language and Myth* (tr. S. Langer; New York: Dover, 1946); M. Eliade, *Cosmos and History: The Myth of the Eternal Return* (tr. W. R. Trask; 1954; repr. New York: Harper & Brothers, 1959); S. E. Hyman, "The Ritual View of Myth and the Mythic," in *Myth: A Symposium* (ed. T. A. Sebeok; 1955; repr. Bloomington: Indiana University Press, 1965) 136-53; C. G. Jung, *Psyche and Symbol* (ed. V. de Laszlo; New York: Doubleday, 1958); C. G. Jung and A. Kerényi, *Essays on a Science of Mythology* (1949; repr. New York: Harper & Row, 1963); G. S. Kirk, *Myth: Its Meaning and Functions in Ancient and Other Cultures* (Cambridge: Cambridge University Press, 1970); C. Levi-Strauss, "The Structural Study of Myth," in *Myth: A Symposium* (ed. T. A. Sebeok; 1955; repr. Bloomington: Indiana University Press, 1965) 81-106; C. S. Lewis, *An Experiment in Criticism* (Cambridge: Cambridge Univeristy Press, 1961) 40-49; Lord Raglan, "Myth and Ritual," in *Myth: A Symposium* (ed. T. A. Sebeok; 1955; repr. Bloomington: Indiana Univeristy Press, 1965) 122-35; P. Ricoeur, *The Symbolism of Evil* (tr. E. Buchanan; New York: Harper & Row, 1967); J. W. Rogerson, *Myth in Old Testament Interpretation* (BZAW 134; Berlin: De Gruyter, 1974); T. A. Sebeok, ed., *Myth: A Symposium* (1955; repr. Bloomington: Indiana University Press, 1965).

NARRATIVE (Erzählung). An account of events or actions in sequential form. It embraces a wide range of genres: (→) myth, (→) history, (→) story, (→) legend, (→) novella, etc.

R. Alter, *The Art of Biblical Narrative* (New York: Basic Books, 1981); R. Scholes and R. Kellogg, *The Nature of Narrative* (New York: Oxford University Press, 1966).

NOVELLA (Novelle). A long prose (→) narrative produced by a literary artisan for his or her own particular purposes.

The structure depends on the ability of the author to develop suspense and resolve it in particular directions. Toward that end, subplots and interweaving motifs provide depth to the major plot line. Even in the major plot, multiple structures can facilitate a wider range of goals than would normally be the case in traditional narrative. Moreover, characterization can develop subtle tones. Thus the entire piece gives the reader a total impression of event as a complex and subtle process. Figures in the process are subordinated to the crucial character of the process itself.

Setting for the novella lies in the literary activity of the author, who may draw on traditional narratives with settings in various institutions. However, the qualifying characteristic of the novella is the unique shape given to the subject matter by the author. In that sense, the novella is not simply a stage in the history of typical traditional material, but an original creation (cf. Genesis 37–47).

A. Jolles, *Einfache Formen* (2nd ed.; Tübingen: Niemeyer, 1958); H. W. Wolff, *Studien zum Jonabuch* (BibS[N] 47; Neukirchen: Neukirchener, 1965).

ORACLE (Orakel). A subgenre of prophecy, consisting of inspired speech cited directly. It was delivered originally at oracular shrines or by inspired prophets. In the Hellenistic age literary oracles were common. The main Judeo-Christian corpus of literary oracles is the Sibylline collection, which is characterized by pseudonymity and *ex eventu* prophecy and is closely related to the "historical" apocalypses.

D. E. Aune, *Prophecy in Early Christianity and the Ancient Mediterranean World* (Grand Rapids: Eerdmans, 1983); J. J. Collins, "The Sibylline Oracles," in *Jewish Writings of the Second Temple Period* (ed. M. E. Stone; Philadelphia: Fortress, 1984).

OTHERWORLDLY JOURNEY (Himmelsreise, Hadesfahrt). A subgenre of (→) apocalypse that reports a visionary's journey to the heavens or netherworld. It typically involves a numbered series of heavens (in Jewish and Christian works), visions of the abodes of the dead, and often a vision of God. Angels serve as guides and interpreters on the journey, but the symbolism is mythic-realistic rather than allegorical. The roots of this genre should be sought in the (→) dream reports of the ancient Near East, where dream travels to the netherworld are attested as early as the Gilgamesh Epic. Otherworldly journeys are widely attested in the Greco-Roman world and are also known in Persian literature.

The Jewish apocalypses of the journey type may be further classified according to their eschatology. *Apocalypse of Abraham* includes an overview of history leading to the eschaton. Some Enochic writings (*Book of the Watchers* in *1 Enoch* 1–36; *2 Enoch*) predict a cosmic judgment, but do not have a review of history, while other works, like *3 Baruch,* have only personal eschatology (the judgment of the individual after death).

C. Colpe, "Die Himmelsreise der Seele ausserhalb und innerhalb der Gnosis," in *Le Origini dello Gnosticismo* (ed. U. Bianchi; Leiden: Brill, 1967) 429-47; M. Himmelfarb, *Tours of Hell: An Apocalyptic Form in Jewish and Christian Literature* (Philadelphia: University of Pennsylvania, 1983); A. F. Segal, "Heavenly Ascent in Hellenistic Judaism, Early Christianity, and their Environments," *ANRW* II.23.2 (1980) 1333-94.

PARENESIS (Paränesis). An address to an individual (or group) that seeks to persuade with reference to a goal. It may be composed of several genre elements and characteristic stylistic features, in a flexible arrangement (cf. Deuteronomy 6–11; Prov 1:8ff.). Hence one finds commands, prohibitions, instructions, etc., mixed into a parenetic address. Parenesis may exhort, admonish, command, or prohibit in its intent to persuade, and motive clauses are frequently included.

PERIODIZATION OF HISTORY (Periodisierung von Geschichte). The division of history, or a significant segment of it, into a set number of periods. It is widespread as a feature of (→) *ex eventu* prophecy in (→) apocalypses, (→) testaments, and (→) oracles of the Second Temple period. This kind of schematization may have been developed under Persian influence. It functions to convey a sense of determinism and of the imminence of the end.

D. Flusser, "The four empires in the Fourth Sibyl and in the Book of Daniel," *Israel Oriental Studies* 2 (1972) 148-75.

PESHER (Pescher). A form of exegetical (→) midrash, attested primarily in the scrolls from Qumran. The commentary is direct and explicit and treats the text piecemeal. The Qumran pesharim proceed systematically from one textual unit to another and introduce the pesher by formulas (e.g., *pšrw 'l*: "its interpretation is concerning . . ."; or *pšrw 'šr*: "its interpretation is that . . .").

The term pesher is also used for the interpretation of dreams and of the writing on the wall in Daniel. The origin of the genre is related to (→) dream interpretation (cf. the Akkadian cognate *pašāru* and the use of *ptr, ptrwn* in the Joseph story in Genesis).

The exegetical midrash on the seventy weeks of Jeremiah in Daniel 9 could also be regarded as a pesher.

Related genre: (→) Midrash.

M. P. Horgan, *Pesharim: Qumran Interpretations of Biblical Books* (CBQMS 8; Washington: Catholic Biblical Association of America, 1979).

PETITION (Petition, Bittrede, Bittschrift). A request or plea from one person to another asking for some definite response. The petition normally includes (1) the basis for the request, and (2) the actual request. Prayers of petition addressed to God are a more elaborate development of this speech form (cf. Psalms 13, 17, 69).

POLITICAL ORACLE (politisches Orakel). A subgenre of (→) oracle that deals with the rise and fall of kingdoms and was very widespread in the Hellenistic age: cf. the Egyptian Potter's Oracle, Persian Oracle of Hystaspes, and Judeo-Christian *Sibylline Oracles*. These oracles may be communicated in dreams or visions and often include (→) *ex eventu* prophecy.

The typical setting of these oracles may be broadly construed as Near Eastern resistance to Hellenism in the Hellenistic age, but the oracles could be adapted to serve other purposes, e.g., *Sibylline Oracles* 11 is pro-Roman. The dream interpretation in Daniel 2 constitutes a biblical political oracle.

J. J. Collins, *The Sibylline Oracles of Egyptian Judaism* (SBLDS 13; Missoula: Scholars Press, 1974); S. K. Eddy, *The King is Dead* (Lincoln: University of Nebraska, 1961); H. Fuchs, *Der geistige Widerstand gegen Rom in der antiken Welt* (Berlin: Weidmann, 1938).

PRAYER (Gebet). An address to a god or gods. This is a macrogenre which encompasses several specific genres with a wide range of purposes and settings. Prayer may be private or public, formal or informal, prose or poetic, direct (second person) or indirect (third person, e.g., "may God deliver you"), and can serve as petition, intercession, expression of praise, thanks, etc. Most psalms are types of prayer.

M. Greenberg, *Biblical Prose Prayer* (Berkeley: University of California, 1983); C. Westermann, *The Praise of God in the Psalms* (tr. K. Crim; Richmond: John Knox, 1965).

PRAYER OF PETITION (Petitionsgebet). A (→) prayer which makes a specific request of God. It may stand alone (e.g., Dan 6:17 [*RSV* 16]) or as a component of a longer prayer (e.g., Dan 9:16-19).

PROCLAMATION (Verkündigung, Proklamation). A public announcement, made or authorized by a person in authority. It may be delivered by a herald or messenger. Cf. Dan 3:4-6; 3:31–4:34 (*RSV* 4:1-37; in epistolary form).
Related genre: (→) Decree.

PROPHECY OF COSMIC TRANSFORMATION (Prophezeiung der Weltallverwandlung). A variant of (→) eschatological prophecy that focuses on the transformation of this world rather than on the judgment of the dead. Cf. Isa 11:1-9; *2 Baruch* 73–74.

REGNAL PROPHECY (Prophezeiung bezüglich Könige). A form of (→) *ex eventu* prophecy that is concerned with the rise and fall of kings. This form is characteristic of a genre of Akkadian prophecy which has been described as follows: "They consist in the main of predictions after the event. . . . The predictions are divided according to reigns and often begin with some such phrase as 'a prince will arise.' Although the kings are never named it is sometimes possible to identify them on the basis of details provided in the 'prophetic' description" (Grayson, 13). A biblical example can be found in Daniel 11. The setting of these prophecies may be broadly construed as political propaganda.
A. K. Grayson, *Babylonian Historical-Literary Texts* (Toronto: University of Toronto Press, 1975); W. G. Lambert, *The Background of Jewish Apocalyptic* (London: Athlone Press, 1978).

REVELATION REPORT (Offenbarungsbericht). A report of the content of a revelation that does not describe the process by which it was received. Cf. *Apocalypse of Weeks* in *1 Enoch* 93:1-10; 91:11-19.

REVELATORY DIALOGUE (offenbarender Dialog, Offenbarung als Dialog). A conversation between a revealer (God, an angel) and a recipient. It is distinguished from other dialogue by the supernatural dialogue partner. There is usually some dialogue in symbolic visions, but revelatory dialogue can also be used independently as a constituent of apocalypses (cf. 4 Ezra, *2 Baruch*). This genre is further developed in Gnosticism.

SIGNS OF THE END (Vorzeichen vom Ende). Stereotyped prediction of upheavals immediately preceding the final judgment (cf. Mark 13:24-25). Antecedents can be found in OT prophecy (Joel 3:3-4 [*RSV* 2:30-31]).
K. Berger, "Hellenistisch-heidnische Prodigien und die Vorzeichen jüdischer und christlicher Apokalyptik," *ANRW* II.23.2 (1980) 1428-69.

STORY (Sage, Erzählung, Geschichte). A (→) narrative that creates interest by arousing tension and resolving it. The structure of a story is controlled by a plot, moving from exposition through complication in relationships between major figures to denouement and conclusion.
The setting for story cannot be controlled, under most circumstances, with as much precision as it can be for other genres. Stories that belong to

popular literature can be told in diverse settings (cultic celebrations, family entertainment, etc.). Perhaps the most dominant setting for story telling is entertainment (cf. Lord). But entertainment can influence people in multiple directions: didactic, ethical, propagandistic, etc.

The story may be independent of all other contexts. If so, it may reveal typical elements of narration identified as a part of folk narrative by Olrik (cf. Genesis 38). Or, the story may function as a typical theme or episode in a larger (→) saga (cf. Exod 2:1-10).

Related genre: (→) Legend.

A. B. Lord, *The Singer of Tales* (New York: Atheneum, 1965); A. Olrik, "Epic Laws of Folk Narrative" (tr. J. P. Steager and A. Dundes), in *The Study of Folklore* (ed. A. Dundes; Englewood Cliffs: Prentice-Hall, 1965) 129-41; C. Westermann, *The Promises to the Fathers: Studies on the Patriarchal Narratives* (tr. D. Green; Philadelphia: Fortress, 1980) 1-94.

SYMBOLIC DREAM VISION (symbolische Traumvision). A nocturnal vision which requires interpretation. The usual pattern involves an indication of the circumstances, description of the vision introduced by a term such as "behold," request for interpretation, interpretation by an angel, and conclusion. Cf. Daniel 7–8; *1 Enoch* 83–84; 85–91; 4 Ezra 11–12; 13; *2 Baruch* 35–47; 53–77.

These visions differ from prophetic symbolic visions such as those in Amos 7–8 by the use of a conventionalized narrative frame, which is typical of (→) dream reports in the ancient Near East. The visions of Zechariah 1–6 are transitional in that they provide a minimal indication of the circumstances. The visions of Zechariah are also much less elaborate than the later apocalyptic visions.

C. Jeremias, *Die Nachtgesichte des Sacharja* (Göttingen: Vandenhoeck & Ruprecht, 1977); K. Koch, "Vom profetischen zum apokalyptischen Visionsbericht," in *Apocalypticism in the Mediterranean World and the Near East* (ed. D. Hellholm; Tübingen: Mohr, 1983) 413-46; S. Niditch, *The Symbolic Vision in Biblical Tradition* (HSM 30; Chico: Scholars Press, 1983).

SYMBOLIC VISION (symbolische Vision). A subgenre of vision report in which the object of the vision must be interpreted. In the oldest examples we find:

(1) announcement of vision
(2) introductory formula: "and behold"
(3) description of vision, often quite brief
(4) question of God to seer
(5) seer's reply and repetition of description
(6) God's explanation of the vision.

Cf. Amos 7:7-9; 8:1-3; Jeremiah 24. In Jer 1:11-12, 13-19 the initial description of the vision is omitted.

The visions of Zechariah represent a transitional stage between these prophetic symbolic visions and symbolic dream visions characteristic of apocalyptic literature.

Related genre: (→) Symbolic Dream Vision.

S. Niditch, *The Symbolic Vision in Biblical Tradition* (HSM 30; Chico: Scholars Press, 1983).

TALE. → Story.

TALE OF COURT CONFLICT (Erzählung von einem Konflict im Hof). A subcategory of (→) court tale with a stereotypical plot:

—The heroes are in a state of prosperity.
—They are endangered, often by conspiracy.
—They are condemned to death or prison.
—They are released for various reasons.
—Their wisdom or merit is recognized and they are exalted to positions of honor.

Such a story can function to entertain or to edify. Cf. Daniel 3; 6; Esther; Joseph in Genesis 37–41.

J. J. Collins, *The Apocalyptic Vision of the Book of Daniel* (HSM 16; Missoula: Scholars Press, 1977) 49-54; A. H. S. Krappe, "Is the Story of Ahikar the Wise of Indian Origin?" *JAOS* 61 (1941) 280-84.

TALE OF COURT CONTEST (Erzählung von einem Streit im Hof). A subcategory of (→) court tale with a stereotypical plot:

—A person of lower status is called before a person of higher status to answer difficult questions or to solve a problem requiring insight.
—The person of higher status poses the problem which no one seems capable of solving.
—The person of lower status solves the problem and is rewarded.

Such a story can function to entertain or to edify. Cf. Daniel 2; Gen 41:1-45.

A. Aarne and S. Thompson, *The Types of the Folktale* (Helsinki: Suomalainen tiedeakatemia, 1964); S. Niditch and R. Doran, "The Success Story of the Wise Courtier: A Formal Approach," *JBL* 96 (1977) 179-99.

TESTAMENT (Testament). A discourse delivered in anticipation of imminent death. The speaker is often a father addressing his sons or a leader addressing his people. The testament begins by describing the situation in which the discourse is delivered and ends with an account of the speaker's death. The actual discourse is delivered in the first person.

Some testaments, notably the *Testaments of the Twelve Patriarchs,* are closely related to the (→) "historical" apocalypses.

J. J. Collins, "Testaments," in *Jewish Writings of the Second Temple Period* (ed. M. E. Stone; Philadelphia: Fortress, 1984); E. von Nordheim, *Die Lehre der Alten. I: Das Testament als Literaturgattung im Judentum der hellenistisch-römischen Zeit* (Leiden: Brill, 1980).

THEOPHANY (Theophanie). Description of the manifestation of a divinity (cf. Exodus 19; Deut 33:2; Judg 5:4-5; Mic 1:3-4; Hab 3:3-6; *1 Enoch* 1:3-7).

Related genre: (→) Epiphany.

Jörg Jeremias, *Theophanie: Die Geschichte einer alttestamentlicher Gattung* (WMANT 10; Neukirchen-Vluyn: Neukirchener, 1965).

THRONE VISION (Thronvision). A vision of God seated on a throne. There is a tradition of such visions in the OT: cf. 1 Kings 22; Isaiah 6; Ezekiel 1.

There is a throne vision in Daniel 7 in an (→) "historical" apocalypse but the main examples are found in (→) otherworldly journeys: cf. *1 Enoch* 14; 60; 71; *Testament of Levi* 5; *2 Enoch* 20–21; *Apocalypse of Abraham* 18. The essential motifs are that God is seated on a throne, surrounded by angels. Other typical motifs are fire and angelic singing.

I. Gruenwald, *Apocalyptic and Merkavah Mysticism* (Leiden: Brill, 1980); C. Rowland, "Visions of God in Apocalyptic Literature," *JSJ* 10 (1979) 138-54.

VISION (Vision). General term for a revelation in visual form. It involves a perception which is distinct from normal sight and is not available for public observation.

Related genres: (→) Symbolic Vision, (→) Symbolic Dream Vision, (→) Dream Report, (→) Apocalypse.

VISIONS OF THE ABODE OF THE DEAD (Visionen vom Verbleib der Toten). A typical constituent of (→) otherworldly journeys (cf. *1 Enoch* 22). These visions are more developed and stereotyped in Christian than in Jewish (→) apocalypses. Visions of the netherworld as the abode of the dead are attested as far back as the Gilgamesh Epic and Homer's *Odyssey,* Book 11.

WISDOM TALE (Weisheitsgeschichte). A (→) story characterized by a moral lesson or by an observation about life such as is characteristic of proverbial wisdom. This category overlaps with other classifications such as (→) court tale or even (→) novella. It is not clearly defined, however, and remains problematic. Possible examples include Esther, Tobit, the tale of Aḥiqar, and 4QPrNab.

S. Talmon, "Wisdom in the Book of Esther," *VT* 13 (1963) 447-51.